Italy

— International boundary
★ National capital
┼┼┼ Railroad
— R

0   50
0

Lambert Confo...

ALG.   8

SWITZERLAND
Bern Lucerne LIECH. Vaduz Innsbruck
Lausanne Geneva
Genova Como Bolzano Tarviso
Chambéry Aosta Trento Udine **SLOVENIA** Klagenfurt **HUNGARY**
FRANCE Novara Bergamo Brescia Vicenza Treviso Ljubljana Zagreb Kaposvar Pécs
Turin Milan Verona Padova Venice Trieste **CROATIA** Osijek
Alessandria Piacenza Po Ferrara Pula Rijeka Karlovac Prijedor Tuzla
Genoa Parma Modena Bologna Ravenna Zadar **BOSNIA AND** Banja Sarajevo
Savona Reggio nell'Emilia Forlì Rimini **HERZEGOVINA** Luka
MONACO La Spezia Massa Prato Florence Pesaro **CROATIA** Split Mostar
Nice Massa Lucca Pisa Arno SAN Ancona
Cannes Livorno MARINO Ploče
Ligurian Bastia Siena Perugia Dubrovnik
Sea Corsica Elba Grosseto *Adriatic* Podgorica
(FR.) Ajaccio Terni Pescara *Sea* Bar
Bonifacio VATICAN Rome Foggia Barletta
Sassari Olbia Latina Andria Bari
Sardinia Naples Salerno Potenza Taranto Brindisi
Cagliari *Tyrrhenian Sea* Lecce
Golfo di Otranto
Taranto
Cosenza
Catanzaro
ISOLE EOLIE *Ionian*
Mediterranean Sea Trapani Palermo Messina *Sea*
Reggio di Calabria
Catania
Sicily Siracusa
Strait of Sicily
TUNISIA *Pantelleria (IT.)*

...negro have asserted
...joint independent state,
...not been formally
...ate by the United States

Italian
AMERICANS

Rebecca Aldridge

CHELSEA HOUSE
PUBLISHERS
A Haights Cross Communications Company

Philadelphia

Frontispiece: Map of Italy with world map inset. Italian immigrants braved a long and difficult journey across the Altantic Ocean for a new and better life in the United States.

CHELSEA HOUSE PUBLISHERS

VP, New Product Development Sally Cheney
Director of Production Kim Shinners
Creative Manager Takeshi Takahashi
Manufacturing Manager Diann Grasse

Staff for ITALIAN AMERICANS

Assistant Editor Kate Sullivan
Production Editor Jaimie Winkler
Picture Researcher Pat Holl
Series Designer Takeshi Takahashi
Cover Designer Takeshi Takahashi
Layout 21st Century Publishing and Communications, Inc.

A Haights Cross Communications Company

http://www.chelseahouse.com

First Printing

1 3 5 7 9 8 6 4 2

Library of Congress Cataloging-in-Publication Data

Aldridge, Rebecca.
   Italian Americans / Rebecca Aldridge.
      p. cm.—(Immigrants in America)
Includes index.
   ISBN 0-7910-7129-4HC   07910-7509-5PB
   1. Italian Americans—Juvenile literature. 2. Italian Americans—History—Juvenile literature. [1. Italian Americans. 2. Immigrants.] I. Title. II. Series: Immigrants in America (Chelsea House Publishers)
E184.I8 A476 2002
973'.0451—dc21

                                                            2002015907

CONTENTS

A NATION OF NATIONS

Daniel Patrick Moynihan

The Constitution of the United States begins: "We the People of the United States . . ." Yet, as we know, the United States was not then and is not now made up of a single group. It is made up of many peoples. Immigrants and bondsmen from Europe, Asia, the Pacific Islands, Africa, and Central and South America came here or were brought here, and still they come. They forged one nation and made it their own. More than 100 years ago, Walt Whitman expressed this great central fact of America: "Here is not merely a nation, but a teeming Nation of nations."

Although the ingenuity and acts of courage of these immigrants, our ancestors, shaped the North American way of life, we sometimes take their contributions for granted. This fine series, IMMIGRANTS IN AMERICA, examines the experiences and contributions of different immigrant groups and how these contributions determined the future of the United States and Canada.

Immigrants did not abandon their ethnic traditions when they reached the shores of North America. Each ethnic group had its own customs and traditions, and each brought different experiences, accomplishments, skills, values, styles of dress, and tastes in food that lingered long after its arrival. Yet this profusion of differences created a bond among immigrants. Ethnic foods, for example, sometimes became "typically" American, such as frankfurters, pizzas, and tacos.

The United States and Canada are unusual in this respect. Whereas religious and ethnic differences have sparked intolerance throughout the rest of the world, North Americans have struggled to learn how to respect each other's differences and live in harmony.

Our two countries are hardly the only two in which different groups must learn to live together. There is no nation of significant size anywhere in the world that would not be classified as multiethnic. But only in North America are there so *many* different groups, most of them living cheek by jowl with one another.

This is not easy. Look around the world. And it has not always been easy for us. Witness the exclusion of Chinese immigrants, and for practical purposes the Japanese also, in the late nineteenth century. But by the late twentieth century, Chinese and Japanese Americans were the most successful of all the groups recorded by the census. We have had prejudice aplenty, but it has been resisted and recurrently overcome.

The remarkable ability of Americans to live together as one people was seriously threatened by the issue of slavery. Thousands of settlers from the British Isles had arrived in the colonies as indentured servants, agreeing to work for a specified number of years on farms or as apprentices in return for passage to America and room and board. When the first Africans arrived in the then-British colonies during the seventeenth century, some colonists thought that they, too, should be treated as indentured servants. Eventually, the question of whether the Africans should be treated as indentured, like the English, or as slaves who could be owned for life, was considered in a Maryland court. The court's calamitous decree held that blacks were slaves bound to a lifelong servitude, and so also were their children. America went through a time of moral examination and civil war before African slaves and their descendants were finally freed. The principle that all people are created equal had faced its greatest challenge and it survived.

Yet the court ruling that set blacks apart from other races fanned flames of discrimination that burned long after slavery was abolished—and that still flicker today. Indeed, it was about the time of the American Civil War that European theories of evolution were turned to the service of ranking different peoples by their presumed distance from our apelike ancestors!

When the Irish flooded American cities to escape the famine in Ireland, the cartoonists caricatured the typical "Paddy" (a common term for Irish immigrants) as an apelike creature with jutting jaw and sloping forehead.

By the twentieth century, racism and ethnic prejudice had given rise to virulent theories of a Northern European master race. When Adolf Hitler came to power in Germany in 1933, he popularized the notion of an Aryan race. Only a man of the deepest ignorance and evil could have done this. *Aryan* is a Sanskrit word taken from the ancient language of the civilizations that inhabited the Indus Valley, which now includes Pakistan and much of Northern India. The term "Aryan," which means "noble," was first used by the eminent German linguist Max Müller to denote the Indo-European family of languages. Müller was horrified that anyone could think of it in terms of a race of blond-haired, blue-eyed Teutons. But the Nazis embraced the notion of a master race. Anyone with darker and heavier features was considered inferior. Buttressed by these theories, the German Nazi state from 1933 to 1945 set out to destroy European Jews, along with Poles, Gypsies, Russians, and other groups considered inferior. They nearly succeeded. Millions of these people were murdered.

The tragedies brought on by ethnic and racial intolerance throughout the world demonstrate the importance of North America's efforts to create a society free of prejudice and inequality.

A relatively recent example of the New World's desire to resolve ethnic friction nonviolently is the solution that the Canadians found to a conflict between two ethnic groups. A long-standing dispute as to whether Canadian culture was properly English or properly French resurfaced in the mid-1960s, dividing the peoples of the French-speaking Province of Quebec from those of the English-speaking provinces. Relations grew tense, then bitter, then violent. The Royal Commission on Bilingualism and Biculturalism was established to study the growing crisis and to propose measures to ease the tensions. As a result of the commission's recommendations, all official documents and statements from the national government's capital at Ottawa are now issued in both French and English, and bilingual education is encouraged. But the commissioners recorded that there were many other groups as well.

Toward the end of the nineteenth century in the United States, public figures such as Theodore Roosevelt began speaking about "Americanism," deploring "hyphenated Americans" as persons only partly assimilated—later it would be said insufficiently loyal—to their adopted country. Ethnicity was seen by many as a threat to national cohesion, and even to national security. During World War I, referring to German Americans, Roosevelt would speak of "the Hun within." During World War II, immigrant Germans and Italians were classified as "enemy aliens," and Japanese Americans were settled in detention camps. With time, however, we became more accepting as ethnicity emerged as a *form* of Americanism, celebrated in the annual Columbus Day and Steuben Day parades, the West Indian parade, the Pakistani parade, and in New York City the venerable St. Patrick's Day parade, which dates back before the American Revolution.

In time, the Bureau of the Census took note. In 1980, for the first time, the census questionnaire asked, "What is this person's ancestry?" In parentheses, it stated: "For example: Afro-American, English, French, German" and so on through a list of 16 possibilities, followed by "etc." The results were a bit misleading. Remember, it was a new question. Census officials now speculate that because the first European group listed was English, many respondents simply stopped there. The result was an "overcount." By 2000, however, the bureau was getting better.

The 2000 census also asked people to identify their ancestry. More than 80 percent chose one or more groups from a list of 89 different groups. Most people "specified," as the census states, a "single ancestry," but almost a quarter cited "multiple ancestry." So which is it: are we a melting pot or a "Nation of nations"? The answer is both. Americans share a common citizenship, which is the most important fact of our civic life. But most also feel part of one group or another, especially recent arrivals.

Of which there are many indeed! Since 1970 more than 26 million immigrants have entered the United States; most immigrants have entered legally, but of late not all. For the longest time, anyone could enter. Under the Constitution, drawn up in 1797, even the trade in African slaves was protected for 20 years—a hideous practice, but well established in Southern states. In time, however, hostility toward newcomers appeared, notably tinged with racial fears. In 1882 an act of U.S. Congress excluded further Chinese immigration, responding to pressure from Californians anxious about "cheap labor." Next there was agitation to exclude Japanese, which only ended when the Japanese government, in what was termed a "Gentleman's Agreement," consented to withhold passports from Japanese emigrants. Restrictions on Asians continued until 1965.

Indeed, at the end of the nineteenth century there was much talk about the "Anglo-Saxon race" and its many virtues. The United States had reached an informal alliance with Great Britain, and we were setting up an empire of our own that included the Philippines, Cuba, Puerto Rico, and Hawaii. Weren't we different from those "others"? Not exactly. Migration has been going on across the world from the beginning of time and there is no such thing as a pure race. The humorist Finley Peter Dunne wrote: "An Anglo-Saxon…is a German that's forgot who was his parents." Indeed, following the departure of the Romans from Britain in the year A.D. 410, Germanic tribes, including Saxons from northern Germany and Anglos from southern Denmark, migrated into the British Isles. In time they defined what we now call Britain, driving the Celts to Wales and Ireland, with an essentially Celtic Scotland to the north.

Thus immigrants from the British Isles, approximately a third of the present day population of the United States, were already a heterogeneous group. Perhaps even more importantly, they belonged to many different religious denominations including the Puritan, Congregational, Episcopalian, Quaker, and Catholic churches, and even a small community of Sephardic Jews from Brazil! No group made up a majority; religious toleration came about largely because there seemed to be no alternative.

American immigration policy developed in much this way. Though completely open at the beginning, over time, efforts were made to limit the influx of certain immigrant groups, in the manner of the exclusion of Asians in the late nineteenth century and the Southern Europeans by the early twentieth century. By the 1960s, however, America was already too diverse to pretend otherwise, and immigration was opened to all nations.

The people of North America are the descendants of one of the greatest migrations in history. And that migration is not over. Koreans, Vietnamese, Mexicans, Nicaraguans, Pakistanis, Indians, Arabs, and many others are heading for the shores of North America in large numbers. This mix of cultures shapes every aspect of our lives. To understand ourselves, we must know something about our diverse ethnic ancestry. Nothing so defines the North American nations as the motto on the Great Seal of the United States: *E Pluribus Unum*—Out of Many, One. ■

1 THE ITALIANS IN AMERICA

DISCOVERING AMERICA

Most Europeans believe that America was a land discovered by Cristoforo Colombo (Christopher Columbus), the son of a weaver who was born in Genoa, Italy. It was Columbus' search for a shorter passage to Asia that led him to unexpectedly "discover" this new land that would later become known as America.

After Columbus, Italian explorers Giovanni Caboto (John Cabot) and Amerigo Vespucci would also set sail for the New World. Neither explorer ever reached America (Cabot in 1497 landed in what is now known as Newfoundland; Vespucci in 1499 was part of a crew that reached what is now known as Brazil), although many years later European mapmakers would use Vespucci's first name, Amerigo, as labels for the two New World continents, North America and South America.

The history of Italians in America dates back to 1492 when Christopher Columbus, the son of a weaver from Genoa, Italy, first set foot on American soil. This engraving shows Columbus before Spain's Queen Isabella, who funded his expeditions.

ITALIAN IMMIGRATION SURGES IN THE 1880s

It might seem that Italians had a major role in the development of the United States; however, by 1871 when Italy was finally one nation with Rome as its capital, only 12,000 to 25,000 Italians were living in America. This number grew rapidly beginning in the 1880s. In the 40 years between 1880 and 1920, almost 4 million Italians came in a mass exodus to the United States looking for hope and fortune. Never before and never since has one ethnic group come to the United States in such large numbers within the same time span. Most of the Italian immigrants were poor southern Italian farmers. In their homeland, these poor Italian farmers had often been at the mercy of wealthy landowners. In America, they would find they would not be treated much better.

Italian immigrants left behind a land that was beautiful

Italian Immigration in Numbers

Italian immigration to the United States, courtesy of United States Immigration and Naturalization Service.

Decade	Number of Immigrants
1821–1830	409
1831–1840	2,253
1841–1850	1,870
1851–1860	9,231
1861–1870	11,725
1871–1880	55,759
1181–1890	307,309
1891–1900	651,893
1901–1910	2,045,877
1911–1920	1,109,524
1921–1930	455,315
1931–1940	68,028
1941–1950	57,661
1951–1960	185,491
1961–1970	214,111
1971–1980	129,368
1981–1990	67,254
1990–2000	25,752
TOTAL	5,398,830

but that offered them little for their efforts. Once in America, they would have to continue their hard work. Instead of toiling away on farms, Italian men would build bridges and skyscrapers. In the words of an Italian immigrant:

> I came to America because I heard the streets were paved with gold. When I got here, I found out three things: first, the streets weren't paved with gold; second, they weren't paved at all; and third, I was expected to pave them.

In keeping with Italian cultural tradition, women and children would work, too, for the betterment of the family lifestyle. Family, along with religion, provided support for these newcomers and helped them survive in the strange new cities of America, where they faced another kind of hard work—fighting prejudice.

HARDSHIPS AND DISCRIMINATION

On their arrival, southern Italians were considered outsiders and faced prejudice and discrimination because of their skin tone, their religion, their customs, and their culture. They were called names such as *dago* and *wop*. They were forced to take pick-and-shovel jobs that no one else would take, digging and tunneling for subways, bridges, and roads. They were even refused admittance to many churches because their religious practices differed from those of the Irish Catholics, who had already established themselves in America.

The new immigrants stuck together and settled in Little Italies, mainly in the cities of New York, Boston, Chicago, and Philadelphia. Here, in these neighborhoods packed with crowded tenement buildings filled with the smells of Italian cooking, they kept their language and the dialects of their provinces, their religious customs, and other traditions from the Old Country to hold them together while they tried to make it in America. All the while, they dreamed of returning to their homeland.

Tracing Your Roots

If you want to learn more about your Italian ancestors, there are a variety of resources to help you research and record your family history. Begin in the present and work into the past, taking accurate and organized notes while you research. Although the names of your ancestors are the most important record on the family tree you will create, it is necessary to add details to distinguish your family members from others.

Detailed records are organized by family groups, sets of parents and their children. This includes birth, marriage, and death dates and their locations for each person. It is possible to print blank charts from genealogy research websites, or you can use free online or downloadable genealogy record programs instead.

Start from your memory, listing yourself, your parents, and your siblings on your blank family group record. Many records such as census, land titles, and birth, marriage, and death certificates list information by county as well as city. Always include county information as you compile your records. Then begin a new family group record for each of your parents, listing their siblings and their parents. Once you have listed as much information as you can remember, ask your relatives to fill in any blanks. It is easiest to work on one family line at a time, such as your maternal grandfather's family.

Your living relatives are a valuable source of information. Their memories and stories are a meaningful part of your family tree. They also will have a great deal of information recorded in family bibles, diaries, letters, photographs, birth certificates, marriage licenses, deeds, wills, and obituary clippings. As you fill in your record, list whether the source of information was a letter, a conversation with your grandmother, or information from your great-uncle's military discharge papers that were stored in the attic. This will make it easier to verify your information.

Local history centers and genealogy societies specialize in assisting people in compiling records and have searchable data such as microfilm census records. Your local library also has many resources. The Internet has made it easy to research your family from home, and there are hundreds of websites for genealogists to access particular information. Many sites allow researchers documenting the same family lines to share their files with another. It is always important to double-check the sources others used to find their information so that you can be sure that your ancestors are truly the same.

A strong sense of family provided essential support for Italian immigrants facing the challenges of a new life in America. Large extended families like this one often lived, worked, and worshipped together in close-knit communities. Here an 80-year-old grandmother visits her relatives in America for the first time.

AMERICANS BY CHOICE

Then, in 1941, something happened that changed the world, especially that of Italian Americans. Japan attacked Pearl Harbor, bringing the United States into World War II. This meant that the U.S. government had officially declared war on the nations of Germany, Japan, and Italy. Italian Americans who had always lived in two worlds now had to make a choice—and they chose to become Americans.

Today, the almost 20 million Italian Americans living in the United States have added more than just flavor to delicious pasta dishes. Among their contributions, they have given song and entertainment, run successful businesses that have strengthened the economy, and influenced the politics of the United States.

2

THE OLD COUNTRY

EARLY HISTORY

Italy is a tall, thin, boot-shaped peninsula that is surrounded by water on three sides: the Tyrrhenian Sea to the west, the Adriatic Sea to the east, and the Ionian and Mediterranean Seas to the south. Italy was not always one nation. After the Roman Empire fell in the fifth century, the land of Italy remained divided, never having one single ruler. Many foreign invaders including Lombards, Byzantine Greeks, Arabs, Normans, Catholic Germans, French, and Spaniards took their turns occupying the land, each establishing permanent settlements. Northern Italy was filled with successful, independent city-states such as Milan, Venice, and Florence.

The north and its successful merchants and bankers interested in art, literature, and science led the Italian Renaissance that lasted

Many Italians arriving in America had worked as farmers in Italy's fertile valleys, which were home to many vineyards and orchards. Although the countryside was beautiful, life in these small Italian farm towns was often difficult, lacking many of the conveniences we take for granted today.

from 1420 to the 1600s. Central Italy included Vatican City, the center of Catholicism, where the pope lived in his palace. The south, known as the Kingdom of the Two Sicilies, was much different from the north where different dialects of Italian were spoken. Mainly farmlands filled this poor land. After 1504, the southern part of the Italian peninsula and the island of Sicily were fiefdoms belonging to Spanish princes, and Spanish rule remained dominant in the south for 200 years.

ALLIANCE OF GIUSEPPE MAZZINI AND GIUSEPPE GARIBALDI

Italians began to dream of a united nation in the beginning of the 1800s. In 1804, Napoleon Bonaparte, the emperor of France, put his brother on the throne of a kingdom of Italy, but this kingdom did not last long. After Napoleon's defeat, Italy was divided again, but its people still believed it could once again be joined together. One of those believers was Giuseppe Mazzini, born in 1805 in Genoa. He founded the organization *Giovane Italia* (Young Italy). Mazzini's goal was to incite a feeling of nationalism among his fellow countrymen and women. He attacked the Catholic Church for its mix of materialism and religion. Mazzini was able to convince many middle-class youths that Italian unity was a religious cause.

A man by the name of Giuseppe Garibaldi later joined Mazzini. Born in Nice (now a part of France, but historically an Italian province) on July 4, 1807, Garibaldi, was the son and grandson of seamen involved in coastal shipping. His mother, a Catholic, was insistent that her son receive an education. At age 15, Garibaldi decided to leave school to become a cabin boy on a Russian ship headed to Odessa (a city on the Black Sea in the Republic of Ukraine). He earned a master's certificate as a sea captain 10 years later. After he joined Mazzini, the two led revolts. When their revolts failed, they were condemned to death and forced to flee from Italy.

Mazzini ended up in London in 1837. He spent much of his adult life there publishing newspapers and pamphlets that still carried the message of freedom to his fellow Italians. Garibaldi fled to Brazil in 1834, where he tried to earn a living as a trader on the Brazilian coast with goods such as sugar, brandy, and flour. After being a tradesman, Garibaldi spent 14 years as a member of the navy of the Brazilian province Rio Grande do Sul. During this time, he earned a reputation as a fighter for freedom. He commanded a ship for Brazilians fighting for their own independence and freed African slaves on a Portuguese ship crossing the Atlantic.

Meanwhile, revolts continued to break out on the Italian peninsula, and in 1848 Mazzini returned, waiting in Milan and hoping that an Italian nation was about to come into existence. Because of angry mobs and fighting in the streets, the pope left Rome, fearing for his safety. At this point, Garibaldi returned when asked to do so by Mazzini, who wanted to fight off the armies that were trying to regain the city of Rome for the pope. Garibaldi led a military group into Rome. Mazzini joined forces with Garibaldi, and they formed an independent republic. However, France soon defeated them, killing or capturing most of Garibaldi's 5,000 men and restoring the pope to power. Once again, Mazzini and Garibaldi were driven from the Italian peninsula.

Garibaldi fled to Staten Island, New York, in 1850 and led the life of a poor immigrant candlemaker. Within nine months, he left the United States for Peru, where he became the skipper of a cargo ship. Three years later, he returned to the United States to skipper another cargo ship. Shortly after that, in 1854, Garibaldi was allowed to return to Piedmont (northern Italy) by Prime Minister Count Camille Cavour with the understanding that he would abstain from any involvement in political activities.

In 1860, the United States was on the verge of Civil War, and Italy was still fighting for unification and independence. In the north was the Kingdom of Piedmont and in the south the Kingdom of the Two Sicilies. The cause of Italian unification had been taken up by Count Camille Cavour, Chief Minister to the king of Piedmont-Sardinia, Victor Emmanuel II. Cavour published a newspaper called *Il Risorgimento* (*The Revival*).

In the mid-1800s, Italy was not one nation at all, but several kingdoms under the influence of Austria, France, and the pope in Rome. Giuseppe Garibaldi, a former seaman (seen here at right), made Italian unification his prime goal. Although Garibaldi's early uprisings failed, resulting in his exile, his later efforts to unify Italy proved a success.

Cavour wanted Italian independence; however, he favored a monarchy over a republic and wanted Victor Emmanuel to be king. Soon, France became Victor Emmanuel's ally. This alliance upset Austria which, at the time, controlled large parts of northern Italy. Fearing the growing power of Victor Emmanuel, Austria declared war on Piedmont-Sardinia in 1859. The French proved strong allies and helped the Piedmontese defeat the Austrians.

Revolts once again occurred on the Italian peninsula. Once again Garibaldi came—this time as general of the south's volunteer army. Garibaldi and his group of 1,000 volunteers, wearing red shirts because they had no uniforms, invaded the island of Sicily. After he gained control there, his army moved north to the mainland. Cavour sent his own army into the papal state to join Garibaldi's army, and soon Rome was the only part of central Italy left under the pope's control. Garibaldi later became an Italian hero, and his picture was hung in the homes and shops of most Italian immigrants in America.

UNIFICATION OF ITALY

In March 1861, Victor Emmanuel became ruler of the Kingdom of Italy, formalizing unification. Ten years later, in 1871, the pope gave up Rome, except for the small area of land known as Vatican City, and Rome became Italy's capital.

This unification was political only, however. One Italian official said in 1870, "Although we have made Italy, we have yet to make Italians." In the south, the new government controlled by northern Italians had brought little in the way of beneficial change and ignored the plight of southern peasants. Instead of trading to survive, peasants now needed money to pay four different taxes. Corrupt officials still governed. Young village men were also required to serve in a national army.

Most southern Italians had no land of their own, and if a man did not own land, he could not vote. Even though the Italian government sold off the Catholic Church's vast land holdings, southern peasants were too poor to buy anything but small pieces of land that could not be profitable. This meant that instead of being virtually controlled by landowners and their overseers, peasants now rented land from wealthy landowners who often took advantage of them and kept them living in poverty. Stealing became a common way to meet needs, and the only people a person could trust were family members.

THE PEASANT SOCIAL SCALE

After unification, peasants in the south turned against one another and created their own social scale. At the bottom of this scale were peasants employed by the gentry. They were followed by day laborers. Slightly higher up the scale were farmers, then those who owned a piece of land, a house, and a donkey. Storekeepers and artisans were at the top of the scale, and they did not really associate with peasants.

LIFE IN THE MEZZOGIORNO

Most people who came to America between the 1880s and 1920s came from the seven regions south of Rome called the Mezzogiorno: Abruzzo, Molise, Campania, Basilicata (then called Lucania), Apulia, Calabria, and Sicily. Each region had its own dialect, folklore, tradition, and patron saints. Even by the year 1860, there was no unifying language in Italy. Only 2.5 percent of the population could speak Italian, all the rest spoke the dialect of their region. For example, the word "cockroach" in Italian was *blatta,* in Tuscan it was *piattola,* in Rome they said *bagherozzo,* in Naples the word was *scarafone,* and in Sicily it was *cacarocielu.*

Under Spanish and Bourbon rule, which lasted for 400 years (the last official Bourbon monarch ruled the south from 1830 to 1839), the Mezzogiorno was kept apart from the rest of the world, and living there was almost like living in medieval times.

The Mezzogiorno has a warm, tropical climate. The summers are dry and hot, and the fall is windy and rainy. Towns and villages contained cube-shaped homes of mud and stone that reached from high ground and moved down to low valleys. Each town had a *piazza* that served as a marketplace and social center with a church at one end and a winehouse at the other.

Each Italian town had a central plaza (or *piazza*) like this one in Florence, which served as a marketplace and social center. In contrast, most Italian homes in the late 1800s were quite small and simple, with a kerosene lamp for light and a stone hearth for cooking.

Here, men strolled arm-in-arm in groups, laughing and chatting through the square. Most people lived in single-story huts. Those who were poor lived in a loft bed above ground, while their animals—a mule, some chickens, and possibly a pig—stayed below. Homes were lighted with a kerosene lamp, and most homes had an oven. Only the very poor needed to cook on stone piles outdoors.

There were few roads and little connection between villages. The streets of the village were usually narrow and made of cobblestone. Often they needed repair. Plumbing did not exist until well into the twentieth century, regardless of whether one was rich or poor. With no sewage system, the villagers typically disposed of human waste directly in the streets.

Southern Italian farmers grew peaches, walnuts, grapes, olives, and wheat. They had no machines to help with planting and harvesting. That meant they did all the work by hand. In Italy, work was more important than school. Education was denied to most of the children living in the region. Usually, only children of the wealthy were allowed to attend school. If children did attend school, they typically left school at age 12 to help the family. Girls helped with household chores; boys took day jobs or worked with their fathers in the fields.

In the summer, southern Italians left their towns and villages to go to their *aria*. This was an airy place in the countryside, usually a simple stone house surrounded by fruit trees and wheat fields.

The food that southerners ate was quite basic: lentils, split peas, or fava beans. For a special occasion, they might add pasta to the mix. Fruit was always on hand and hearty bread was a staple of their diet. Even those of modest means—not the poor—ate meat only two times a year.

HARDSHIPS

Entertainment was quiet and simple. For women, talking and arranging visits were their main sources of entertainment. For men, strolling through the piazza was a way to pass the time. They also met in the piazza to exchange news, ideas, gossip, and to debate issues of common concern. The village's big event was a festival dedicated to the town's patron saint, a time when everyone celebrated. According to one

Italian immigrant who talked about his life back in Sicily, there was little time for play:

> My family was very poor. I never went to school. I started working from before I was ten years old. My father and mother, they send me to work to make maybe ten cents a day. I was working in a lemon factory. I work from one o'clock in the morning to about two in the afternoon the next day. Eleven, twelve hours. Them days, if you make ten cents a day, that was a lot of money. There was no time for play. For fun, I play boccie or soccer maybe. But we have no ball. So we used a lemon.

After *Risorgimento,* the fight for unification, the southern region's conditions worsened. The peasants called this time *La Miseria* or the sorrows. Farming was not easy. Because of previous invasions in which trees had been burned, the topsoil was dry and dusty; so the rich soil underneath just washed away. In addition, southern Italy could not compete with other countries that had more advanced farming methods.

The country's population was increasing rapidly, which meant there was not enough work, food, and land to go around. The poverty level was high, and southern Italy probably had the highest mortality (death) rate in central Europe.

Malaria was rampant. Even as late as 1904, malaria killed about 20,000 people per year in Italy. Landowners had cut down forests to provide timber and cleared land for farming. This practice of clear-cutting caused the soil to erode and created swampland that brought swarms of malarial mosquitoes. Between 1884 and 1887, a series of cholera epidemics (cholera causes severe diarrhea and dehydration) also swept through the land, causing the deaths of 55,000 people.

A number of natural disasters wreaked havoc on the land as well. From 1839 to 1872, Mount Vesuvius, a volcano in southern Italy, erupted six times. And from 1852 to 1900, regular eruptions of another volcano, Mount Etna in Sicily, destroyed

Italy is home to two active volcanoes, Mount Vesuvius and Mount Etna. During the late 1800s, each experienced a series of eruptions that devastated villages, killed farm animals, and destroyed crops. Here, villagers near the foot of Mount Etna gather to pray as lava approaches their town.

crops and villages and caused the death of many animals and people. Italy has also known the effects of pestilence. Phylloxera, an insect that is a close relative to the aphid, came came to Italy, destroying many of the country's lush vineyards. There were also droughts and earthquakes. One earthquake shook the land at the same time that a tidal wave hit and destroyed most of the Sicilian province of Messina and part of Calabria. About 100,000 people died as a result of this combined disaster.

Italians had started hearing stories of America from travelers who came back and told them what the country was like. From what they had heard, southern Italians started envisioning America as a dream place, a paradise on earth. It sounded like an escape from the miseries they were suffering in their own country.

By this time, southern Italian immigrants felt little loyalty toward their homeland. They worked land owned by others. By 1900, 65 percent of all land in Italy belonged to land barons. These barons might own from 3,000 to 18,000 acres of land, mostly in the south. Generally, the overseers of this land knew nothing of farming techniques, crop rotation, and soil conservation.

La Miseria was defeating the land and the southern Italians. They felt a drive to defeat poverty, and so far a united Italy had brought them nothing. Paulina Caramando, an immigrant in 1920 at age 8, described the hardships of living in Italy:

> We had no running water. There was a fountain with faucets in the town where we used to wash our clothes. We had these rocks, and we would use that for a scrub board. . . . We would also fill clay jugs with water to take home. People would [carry] it on their head. And everybody had a donkey and they'd take their animals down there to water them. To go to the bathroom, we'd dig a hole in the garden. That's all there was. Not even an outhouse. You just squatted down and that was that . . .

Only one solution seemed possible to improve their situation—leave and try their luck in America.

Their reasons for leaving were to escape poverty and persecution, and they longed for the promise of a better life. In 1878, an Italian government official sent out a decree

Italian Proverbs

When Italian immigrants came to the United States they brought their culture and traditions with them. What follows is a sampling of some of the better known proverbs that Italian immigrants brought to their new home.

Tale padre, tale figlio.	Like father, like son.
L'unità fa la forza.	Unity makes strength.
Ride bene chi ride l'ultimo.	He who laughs last laughs best.
L'abito non fa il monaco.	Clothes don't make the man. (Literally: The habit does not make the monk.)
Pura regina avutu bisogno era vicina.	Even a queen needs a neighbor.
Roma non fu fatta in un giorno.	Rome wasn't built in a day.
Lontano dagli occhi, lontano dal cuore.	Out of sight, out of mind. (Far from the eyes, far from the heart.)
Ogni spicchju è spacchju.	Every little bit helps.
Volere è potere.	Where there's a will, there's a way. (To want is to be able.)
Non c'è due senza tre.	When it rains, it pours. (There are not two without three.)
Chi dorme non piglia pesci.	The early bird catches the worm. (One who sleeps doesn't catch fish.)
Prendere due piccione con una fava.	To kill two birds with one stone. (To catch two pigeons with one bean.)
Dimmi con chi vai or ti diro chi sei.	A man is known by the company he keeps. (Tell me who you go with and I'll tell you who you are.)
Oggi in figura, domani in sepoltura.	Here today, gone tomorrow. (Today in person, tomorrow in the grave.)
Fra il due mali, scegli il minore.	Between two evils, choose the lesser.

urging his people not to leave their nation. In response, a group of peasants said:

> What do you mean by a nation, Mr. Minister? Is it the throng of the unhappy? Aye, then we are truly the nation. . . . We plant and we reap wheat but never do we eat white bread. We cultivate the grape but we drink no wine. We raise animals for food but we eat no meat. We are clothed in rags. . . . And in spite of all this, you counsel us, Mr. Minister, not to abandon our country. But is that land, where one cannot live by toil, one's country?

The rush to America had begun.

3 THE JOURNEY TO AMERICA

IMMIGRANTS FROM NORTHERN ITALY

The major wave of Italian immigrants to the United States came from southern Italy during the 1880s to the 1920s. However, they were not the first Italian immigrants to come to America. Between 1820 and 1870, about 25,000 Italians came to the United States, most emigrating from northern Italy. In 1850, the United States census showed that Louisiana had the largest population of Italian Americans living within its boundaries. Most of these newly arrived Louisiana residents earned a living by fishing and farming. But not all of these Italian immigrants were settling in the southern part of the country. In fact, beginning with the California Gold Rush in 1848, San Francisco's North Beach, located between Telegraph Hill and Russian Hill, became a center for Italian immigrants. Most of these immigrants came from

Unlike the immigrants from Italy's northern regions, who came to America in the early ninteenth century, those arriving from the southern provinces between 1880 and 1920 had little money, education, or skills. Upon their arrival, many were forced to take menial jobs as laborers. Here, Italian railroad workers stand beside their sod huts.

northern Italy as well. One Italian immigrant said of the California Gold Rush, "If California hadn't been so far away from Italy all the Italians would have gone in search of heaven." By 1860, California had 2,805 Italian Americans residing there—more than in any other state. Some stayed after the Gold Rush to work orchards and vineyards. They enjoyed the climate, which was similar to the one they had left behind.

In the early 1800s, other Italian immigrants found their way to the silver mines of Colorado, Wyoming, and Arizona. Some settled in logging camps in Washington state.

Early settlements of Italian immigrants were also located in New York and Chicago.

Northern Italians had a tradition of immigration to America that dated back to the 1600s. The very first group of Italian immigrants to make their way from Italy to New York were Italian Protestants. The group came in 1657 seeking escape from religious persecution and settled in the Dutch colony of New Amsterdam (later called New York).

However, the northern Italians' reasons for leaving were much different from those of the poorer southern Italians. Many northerners already had money and came to America as doctors, lawyers, and merchants. They were considered cultured and sophisticated and were treated much differently from the way their southern counterparts would be treated later. Some northern Italians merely came for adventure or just to see the New World. Others were artists, sculptors, and stoneworkers, or people skilled in other desirable trades. After they arrived, some opened schools and taught music and art. Because of the turmoil in Italy, some of the first early immigrants were political exiles.

IMMIGRANTS FROM SOUTHERN ITALY

The first southern Italians to come to America starting in the 1880s were mainly from the provinces of Sicilia, Calabria, and Campania. They began what has been the greatest mass exodus from a country in human history, and their journey was not an easy one. Southern Italian immigrants were mostly poor farmers, who dreamed of making a better life for their Italian families. Often, these Italian families were the ones that they left in the Old Country while trying to gain wealth in America, a land they believed was full of opportunity.

GETTING TO PORT

Before any Italian could leave the country, he or she had to get a *nulla osta*. This document stated that there were no legal reasons why the person could not leave the country. For example, the person had no military obligations to keep him from going. Once all documentation was in order, the local priest would celebrate Mass as a way to guarantee the emigrant a safe journey across the ocean and success in America.

Many emigrants traveled by foot—sometimes walking 40 or 50 miles—to a port city such as Palermo, Naples, or Genoa, where they would take an ocean liner across the Atlantic to America. Often, this was an emigrant's first experience seeing a city, aside from possibly having taken produce to nearby towns to sell in the marketplace.

For longer trips to a port city, Italians rode a donkey, or if they had enough money, they traveled by train.

Trips to the port city alone could cost more than expected. Expenses included transport, food, and lodging. Sometimes emigrants were taken advantage of in these port cities. If not careful, they could spend their money before even leaving the country. Agents wanting to make extra money sent emigrants to the port city early so they had to pay for extra meals and lodging. Con artists tried to take advantage of emigrant travelers several ways. They would sell "American clothes," presumably to help the emigrant fit in once they arrived in the new land. They also sold false certificates for smallpox vaccinations and the eye disease trachoma. Some dishonest men even dressed as monks and sold pictures and cards with the images of saints on them to ensure the emigrants' safe passage. One dentist claimed the long sea voyage would cause terrible toothaches and for a fee offered to extract the possibly troublesome teeth. Then there were the "porters," who would offer to take an emigrant's bags directly to his or her cabin and then disappear—the emigrant's belongings never to be seen again.

BIRDS OF PASSAGE

The first to make the trip to *Lamerica,* as the Italian immigrants called it, were men between the ages of 16 and 45. These were single men and men who left their wives and children behind, hoping to return to Italy later with enough money for a successful, happy life. These men became known as "birds of passage." They left Italy to make money in America. They might go back and forth between the two countries three or four times. For example, they might go to America, stay and work for five or six years, return to Italy with money, live in Italy for a while, then need more money, go back to America, and so on. Of course, this caused much sadness in families who were separated. Salvatore Castagnola, who eventually emigrated with his mother and siblings from Sicily to Brooklyn, recalls such sadness in his family:

> Whenever we received a letter from America, mother cried for several days . . . Always speculating on what my father was doing at the moment in far away America. "There is a difference of six hours between Italy and America," my mother would say, "It is now eight o'clock, it must be two in the morning in Brooklyn of America. Your father must be asleep dreaming of us."

Some Italian women became known as *vedova biance* or "white widows." These women were still married, but their husbands married again in the United States, starting a whole new family and abandoning the wife back in Italy. The women left behind were often young, strong, and healthy. Many had been married to their husbands for only a short time.

When many of these men did return to Italy with wealth in hand, the rush to America began. Soon others were making their way to the United States. The largest percentage was from rural districts. These men perhaps owned some land but not enough to provide their family with a decent livelihood.

My America

"When we got to Ellis Island, I went one way and my family went another. I don't know what happened to them. They brought me to the hospital. I was there for twenty-three days.

"My sisters, with my father and mother, went to Pennsylvania. My father had to pay a $250 bond that he would return to get me.

"I wanted my mother. I was crying when they got me. There were two men that brought me into the hospital. I was kicking and screaming and after a while I got tired, and they put me in there with this girl who was older than I was. She must have been about thirteen, fourteen. 'Me Jew,' she said. She didn't speak Italian. I remember we got a kick out of the sliced bread in the morning when they brought us breakfast, and we would both talk with our hands, and try to make each other understand. She only stayed about a week with me, because then I was left alone in there.

"Nobody told me anything. Nobody explained, nobody ever said a word to me for twenty-three days. Just the nurse that came in and took my temperature. . . .

"When I got home, there was a really big feast and I asked my mother what happened, and she said she didn't know anything. The next day, they made sure that I enrolled in school, and they had me go in the first grade. I was too smart for the first grade, you know. But I couldn't pronounce the words properly. Like the A here, was 'ah' there, you know, C, 'chi.' So it was different. And there were no other immigrant kids in my class, so the kids used to make fun of me, call me 'dago.' Call me all different kinds of names. And, for a while, I wouldn't go to school no more. I stayed home. Then I was sent back, but I didn't go much. I only had three years of schooling in America. . . .

"One [of my sisters] met the fellow next door and she got married when she was sixteen. The only way she met this boy was because he lived next door. My eldest sister, the dressmaker, went to New York six months after we got to Pennsylvania and got married right away. So at thirteen I was left with my mother. I had to help her with the babies. She had six. One died, but she had five living. I was like a little mother. I had already quit school, and no woman worked in Pittstown. No woman could go to work whether they were willing or not. Only men were allowed to work.

"So, when I was sixteen, I came to New York. I told my father I was going to see my aunt. I never went back."

— Angelina Palmiero, who emigrated from Sicily in 1923 at age 10

Included in this group were tenant farmers, field workers, and shepherds. Often they were not the poorest of the poor, but they left because they feared falling into poverty. Another 20 percent of immigrants were fishermen and artisans, such as masons, carpenters, stonecutters, bakers, blacksmiths, shoemakers, tailors, and miners. A small percentage or immigrants consisted of tradesman, entrepreneurs, doctors, lawyers, teachers, and pharmacists. A young man might have left for personal reasons, perhaps to escape his father's dominance, perhaps to forget being jilted by a girl whom he had planned to someday marry.

When referring to taking a chance in America, Italian immigrants used the expression, "You've got to have luck in this world." One report even states that an entire Sicilian village left for America at the same time. They left the landowner they worked for a note that read: "Sir, do your farming yourself—we are going to America."

THE TRIP

Unfortunately, the trip to America was not an easy one, and many immigrants called it *via dolorosa* or sorrowful way. The 4,000-mile sea voyage took two weeks and was spent aboard an ocean liner that held up to 6,000 passengers. Unlike first- or second-class passengers, Italian immigrants spent their time in steerage class, which meant traveling in the cargo space one or two stories below deck in unhealthy ship holds right next to the ship's steering equipment. Sometimes they shared the space with horses or cattle. It meant breathing foul air on ships that smelled of human waste. Each compartment below deck held 300 people. Often there was only saltwater to wash with. The immigrants spent two weeks being seasick, and disease was common. Many passengers in the dark confines below deck feared the ship would sink, and many screamed prayers to their patron saints to bring them safely to America.

When the weather was good, the immigrants took turns—one time each day—crowding onto the deck for fresh air. To pass the time, young passengers sang and played mouth organs, tambourines, accordions, mandolins, and guitars. When the seas were quiet, they danced. Immigrants played traditional card games such as *scopa* and *briscola*.

Unfortunately, the food was barely edible; the immigrants might be served soup out of huge metal tanks and given stale bread. The food was only enough to keep them alive; so, many immigrants brought along food of their own to help keep up their strength during the voyage. The crew did not treat those in steerage class kindly—often yelling at them for one reason or another.

INEFFECTIVE REGULATIONS TO IMPROVE CONDITIONS ABOARD SHIP

In 1902, the Passenger Act was passed, requiring that chairs and tables be provided for each class aboard ship—including steerage. However, in 1904 Adolfo Russo charged on behalf of the Italian Immigration Office that this regulation to prevent overcrowding was being ignored. An investigation by U.S. authorities showed that 90 percent of ships were in violation of the regulation and that not a single violation had been recorded in the annual reports of the U.S. Immigration Bureau. Six years later, another even more thorough investigation showed that steerage conditions had not improved.

ELLIS ISLAND

Once Italian immigrants reached New York Harbor, they saw the Statue of Liberty, the symbol of freedom and hope. One immigrant remembered her first sight of the statue, "And somebody yelled, 'The Statue of Liberty, the Statue of Liberty!' We all ran to the railing to see, and everybody was praying and kissing and happy that we were coming up the Hudson. . . . "

Once Italian immigrants reached the shores of America, their worries were not over. The lengthy wait for processing at New York's Ellis Island was often followed by an often longer wait (sometimes days) for a ferry to take them across the last mile of water to the city.

The immigrants' worries, however, were certainly not over. First- and second-class passengers were the first allowed off the ocean liner and onto the ferryboats waiting to take them to Ellis Island. From Ellis Island, it was only another mile to the mainland of America. The Italian immigrants of steerage class, however, sometimes had to wait days before a ferry could take them to Ellis Island.

To Italian immigrants, Ellis Island became known as *isola della lacrime* or Island of Tears because the experience was so emotional. Of the 12 million people who passed through Ellis Island from the time it opened in 1892 to 1924 when new laws restricted immigration into the United States, one-third were Italian.

LANDING STATION AT CASTLE GARDEN

Prior to the opening on Ellis Island in 1892, however, immigrants headed right off the ship and onto the streets of New York, where they were quickly surrounded by "runners." These runners were often employees of board-inghouses and travel agencies, who quoted low rates for their employer's services. Once the newly arrived immigrant had agreed to pay the fee quoted by the runner, the immigrant might later learn that the fee was not what was quoted. Frightened with the threat of police involvement, the immigrant would usually pay what was demanded, rather than risk the possibility of questioning or arrest by the police.

Prior to the opening of immigration stations, many immigrants lost money to these schemes, forcing New York City officials to open a landing station in 1855. The station was called Castle Garden. It was first built as a fortress in 1807 to protect Manhattan from foreign invasions. Later, Castle Garden became an amusement center and opera house, where Americans first attended performances of Italian opera. At Castle Garden, new immigrants could safely exchange foreign money, buy railroad tickets, and get information about lodging and employment from social agencies. However, when the number of immigrants entering the United States grew larger in the late 1800s, emphasis changed from helping new immigrants to weeding out the undesirables, and in 1890 the federal government took over the immigration process.

THE REGISTRATION PROCESS AT ELLIS ISLAND

Where the Castle Garden process had been helpful, the Ellis Island process was often confusing, humiliating, and sometimes frightening for new immigrants. During its peak, Ellis Island saw as many as 5,000 people arrive each day. There were approximately 600 staff members for the 5,000 immigrants. Once the immigrants arrived on the island, they were separated into groups of 30. Each person had a number pinned onto his or her clothing for identification. From there they were led into the massive Registry Hall, which some likened to being penned like cattle. Here, they waited in long lines with their luggage.

Physical Examination

Immigration processing required that all third-class and steerage passengers—but not first- and second-class passengers—obtain physical exams. Such exams could be as quick as 45 minutes if there was no overcrowding, or as long as three to four hours. If an immigrant showed signs of a disease, examiners put a chalk letter on his or her clothing. Just some of the chalk marks an immigrant might receive included an E, which meant eyes; an H, which meant possible heart trouble; an L, which meant "lameness"; a P, which meant lungs. PG stood for pregnancy; a circled X meant a suspected mental disability; an F meant a bad rash on the face.

Examiners then determined whether marked immigrants had a condition that warranted deportation. About half the immigrants received at least one mark or another. This process was not scientific, and a cough or limp might be enough to send them back to Italy, but only about two percent were actually deported. One of the worst parts of the medical examination was the eye exam in which a metal instrument was used to pull back the eyelid and check for a disease called trachoma (a contagious bacterial infection of the eyes that

Health inspections at Ellis Island were often painful and humiliating. The eye exam (shown here) used a metal instrument to pull back the eyelid to check for trachoma. Those testing positive for the disease were usually deported.

can cause blindness if not treated). If immigrants showed signs of this disease, they got an E marked on their coat and were usually deported. Receiving any one of the chalk letters meant a closer examination.

One immigrant recalled his arrival at Ellis Island and part of the medical exam:

When we reach New York, I thank the good Lord. It was early morning, the Fourth of July. We was on the deck like a bunch of sheep. Everybody had a suitcase, dragging their suitcase, and I remember the first meal they gave to us at Ellis Island. They give a sandwich, white bread with a piece of cheese and a piece of ham and it tasted so good. It tasted like a nice piece of cake. That was something new for me. I never seen sandwiches in Sicily. They examined if you had lice in your head. If you did, they shaved your hair. I remember that. There was a lot of bald people. And if you had some kind of disease in your eye, they send you back.

An immigrant needing further examination might be kept several days at Ellis Island. On an average night in 1907, 1,700 women and children might be squeezed into a dormitory meant to sleep only 600 people. If an immigrant received a chalk mark and was allowed to stay in America but needed treatment, he or she would have to stay at the Ellis Island hospital before being admitted into the United States.

If a single member of a family did not pass the physical exam, the family had a tough decision to make. Should they all proceed to America without that family member, or should they all return to Italy together? Sometimes if the parents did not pass the physical exam but the children did, the parents would send their children on to be cared for in America by a relative or friend, hoping that life for them in America would be better than in Italy, even without their parents.

Interrogation

After the medical examination came a barrage of questions from a final inspector. In two minutes, immigrants might be asked as many as 38 questions. "What type of immigration are you requesting—temporary or permanent?" "What are your skills and previous occupation?" "Can you read or write?" "What is your country of origin?" "How old are you?" "Who is waiting for you in America?" If an inspector was not satisfied with an answer, immigrants were sent to a special inquiry line with a courtroom-like setting. Here, immigrants were either approved or denied entry to America and deported.

Two questions were of most concern to immigrants. One was "Did you pay for your own passage or was your passage paid for by another person or by any corporation, society, municipality, or government?" And, if yes, "by whom?" This question confused many immigrants because steamship agents and officials instructed them to answer no. The other question was about whether the immigrant "by reason of any offer, solicitation, promise or agreement, expressed or implied, agreed to perform labor in the United States?" Again, they had been told by others to say no.

The two questions stemmed from an attempt by the U.S. government to abolish the *padrone* system. A House Investigating Committee had described this system in which men from America searched Italy for laborers, which often led immigrants to almost slave-like conditions in the United States. These unfortunate laborers would be expected to pay back twice the amount of their passage to America, which could take years. In 1885, legislation made it illegal to import workers under any type of contract. However, *padroni* found it easy to get around these contract labor laws by making verbal agreements rather than written ones.

Money

Another hard question immigrants faced at the final inspection was about money. Between 1885 and 1887, the U.S. Congress passed laws banning immigrants from entering the country who were suspected of being "public charges" or welfare recipients. So immigrants were asked, "Avete monito?" or "Do you have any money?" Some immigrants did not know how best to answer this question. Was it better to have money or not to have money? They might mumble something, say nothing, or contradict themselves. In fact, immigrants needed to show they had some money to get into the country. This posed a problem because often they were leaving Italy to escape poverty and to build a new life for themselves.

Immigrants were usually required to show $20 to $40 per person. Often, immigrants pooled their money, then passed on the same wad of money to the next friend or relative trying to make it into the country. One immigrant wrote in his diary about just such an experience when he arrived in 1906:

> Ascending a small staircase, I reached a desk where I had to declare my money. I came here to make money, but you first have to have money to get into America. I showed the man the three *napoleoni* coins I had borrowed, and he allowed me to proceed.

Escape and Suicide

Some people who were frustrated with the Ellis Island experience and fearing deportation tried to swim to New Jersey. When their bodies were found, they were taken back to Ellis Island and cremated. Suicide was not uncommon for those ordered for deportation. Over the course of 40 years, at least 3,000 immigrants committed suicide on Ellis Island. A young Ellis Island interpreter, Fiorello La Guardia, later ran for public office and became famous as mayor of New York City. His experience at Ellis Island had a profound effect on him and influenced him in his political life. La Guardia once said, "I never managed during the three years I worked there to become callous to the disappointment and despair I witnessed almost daily . . ."

Stairs of Separation

After successfully passing through the final inspection of questions, immigrants came to "The Stairs of Separation." The stairs marked "New York Outsides" took immigrants to a ferry that docked at the southwestern tip of Manhattan Island, where their sponsors (friends or relatives) were waiting for them. The stairs marked "Railroads" brought immigrants to a ferry that would take them to a railroad station in Hoboken, New Jersey; from there they would travel to other parts of the United States such as Florida, Minnesota, and California. The stairs marked "New York Detained" took immigrants to a place where they could wait for their sponsor to pick them up. If a sponsor did not arrive, they would be sent back to Italy.

On average, newly arrived immigrants had five Italians anxiously waiting to greet them. Crowds could get unruly, and from time to time the headlines of New York newspapers would read "Riot of Italians at the Battery." Still, this day was probably a happy one for many immigrants, but once they had arrived in America, Italian immigrants had a whole new life to build.

CHAPTER

4

LAND OF THE
DOLCI DOLLARI

The city was strange and crowded with buildings. Its size was intimidating. Most Italian immigrants did not know English and needed the help of other immigrants. *Paesani* were people they knew from the old country who would take them in and help them find jobs. A *paesano* (or *paesana*), however, could be anyone who looked Italian. An Italian immigrant's first common words were necessary words such as bread, milk, water, and work-related words.

"Italglish" was a mix of English and Italian that only Italian immigrants and those Americans who worked with them could understand. Italglish even helped Italian immigrants understand each other because in Italy they had regional dialects that made it hard for Italians to understand each other once in America. Some examples of Italglish include *giobba* (jahb-uh), which

Though many Italian immigrants had come to America in hopes of earning good wages, a large number were forced to take pick-and-shovel jobs—digging ditches, mines, or subway tunnels.

meant job and *ticcia* (teach-uh), which meant teacher.

The main reason Italian immigrants came to the United States was to find work and make money. Because of the little money they brought with them to America, most needed to find work in the city where they settled. Most did not want to follow the same unsuccessful farming path they had taken in

Italy. That left most Italian immigrants with the jobs no one else would take. Most of these were referred to as pick-and-shovel jobs.

WORK IN NEW YORK CITY

Between 1860 and 1920, the United States was thriving and expanding. During those years, the United States went from being the fourth-largest manufacturing power in the world to the first. The total number of factory workers rose from about 2 million in 1869 to more than 6 million in 1914. Railroads were needed to transport goods across the country. Booming cities needed new streets and buildings. Production in mines and factories was on the rise. So, workers were needed to do heavy labor such as building subways, roads, railroads, and skyscrapers. An example of the hard work of Italian immigrants is their help in building New York's rapid transit system between 1900 and 1930. The New York transit system is the largest such system in the United States. New York City was especially in need of this labor. Between 1880 and 1930, the city was the nation's fastest-growing urban center. One city official even stated, "We can't get along without Italians. We want someone to do the dirty work." So in the city, immigrants often found work digging and building skyscrapers, bridges, tunnels, subways, and streets. Outside the city, they worked on railroads, at quarries, in mines, and in construction.

THE PADRONE SYSTEM

The feeling of being lost in the city and the feeling of helplessness it caused led to the *padrone* system. *Padroni* were Italian-American labor recruiters who placed newly arrived immigrants in jobs. Often they exploited the immigrants and tried to profit from their feelings of helplessness. They found them hard jobs for little pay.

A 15-year-old Italian immigrant describes the conditions

of working for a *padrone* who found him a job on a railroad gang:

> Sharply at five o'clock the boss leaped from his car and began cursing at the men. The poor laborers trembled and hurried. In a moment five hand cars were on the rails. After riding six miles, we arrived at our destination. Amid more cursing the men took the cars off the track and began to tear up the old rails. In a few seconds the sweat was rolling in streams. . . . "The beasts," said the *padrone*, "must not be given a rest, otherwise they will step over me." . . . With nothing but coffee in the morning and bread at noon, these men worked for ten hours every day under the blistering sun or in pouring rain. Stopping work at four, the men returned to their ramshackle cars to cook, eat, and sleep.

Usually, a padrone knew at least more English than the immigrants themselves and acted as an agent, making deals, getting them housing, and taking a large agent's fee—sometimes as much as 60 percent of an immigrant's wages. Often, padroni got immigrants jobs that earlier immigrants, such as the Germans or Irish, would no longer take. These jobs included typical pick-and-shovel jobs, such as digging sewage and water pipelines and building skyscrapers and bridges.

Padroni often were paid to hire workers for certain projects and direct them to that particular work site. Another padrone would then pay the immigrants their meager wages and make sure they worked hard. Some padroni even went to Italy to recruit workers there, paying for their passage to America. Padroni charged the immigrants a lot of money for food and living expenses. They could get away with this because they had a better understanding of the English language than the immigrant did. The padrone system was informal, and some immigrants worked their way in simply by learning English. Padroni also did banking for immigrants and wrote their letters. Padroni saved the Italian immigrants' money for them,

How Others Saw Them

"His [the Italian's] ignorance and unconquerable suspicion of strangers dig the pit into which he falls. He not only knows no word of English, but he does not know enough to learn. Rarely only can he write his own language. Unlike the German, who begins learning English the day he lands as a matter of duty, or the Polish Jew, who takes it up as soon as he is able as an investment, the Italian learns slowly, if at all. Even his boy, born here, often speaks his native tongue indifferently. He is forced, therefore, to have constant recourse to the middle-man, who makes him pay handsomely at every turn. He hires him out to the railroad contractor, receiving a commission from the employer as well as from the laborer, and repeats the performance monthly, or as often as he can have him dismissed. In the city he contracts for his lodging, subletting to him space in the vilest tenements at extortionate rents, and sets an example that does not lack imitators. The 'princely wages' have vanished with his coming, and in their place hardships and a dollar a day, beheft with the padrone's merciless mortgage, confront him. Bred to even worse fare, he takes both as a matter of course, and, applying the maxim that it is not what one makes but what he saves that makes him rich, manages to turn the very dirt of the streets into a hoard of gold, with which he either returns to his Southern home, or brings over his family to join in his work and in his fortunes the next season."

— From "The Italian in New York" in
How the Other Half Lives *by Jacob Riis, published in 1890*

"The Italians are a great expense to this country; they are in all branches of crime and are responsible for most of the crime in this country . . . I have an intimate knowledge of their family life; it was terrible. The young ones mix freedom with license. They get inflated when they find they can walk up and down the street without a soldier putting his hand on their shoulder. The state will have to take care of these criminals. There is too much indifference. They should be put on farms under supervision. It is of vital importance to the welfare of the state. The Italian idea is to get something for nothing. . . . "

— a New Haven, Connecticut inventor c. 1900

"Yes, but where would we find an honest Italian American?"

— President Richard Nixon in a Watergate tape

offering no interest in return. A padrone could then invest that money or deposit it in a savings account as he wished and keep the interest himself. But as Italian immigrants became more familiar with the American way of doing things, padroni were no longer needed.

NEW OCCUPATIONS IN AMERICA

No matter what their jobs had been in Italy, most immigrants found themselves in new occupations in America. There was little availability for anything other than common laborers, so teachers, lawyers, and store owners became miners, factory workers, and shoe shiners.

Money was a necessity, and education took a back seat to work. Italian immigrants had a strong work ethic (a belief that work is a moral good), and it was common to get only as much education as was needed to perform and hold a job.

To survive, all members of the family had to work. One female immigrant explained her family's situation:

> We were here only about a week and my father says to me, "Come on, you have to start traveling with me. I have to show you all the trains. You have to get to work." He needed help. I wasn't supposed to go to work, not even fifteen, but I was the oldest girl. He needed help so bad, I went to work. He took me to New York eight days later after we arrived here.

Men took just about any kind of work they could find. They might find work as a stonemason, shoemaker, fisherman, or skilled laborer if that was what they had done in Italy, but most jobs were not pleasant. Men had the choice of jobs such as garbage collectors or ditch diggers. If not working a pick-and-shovel job, a man might travel as an organ grinder, playing music on a portable machine. Immigrants might work as peddlers, selling goods from pushcarts throughout immigrant neighborhoods. This job itself could be very hard. One immigrant talked about his father, who was a pushcart peddler:

> He had to go to the regional market and the farmers market in the morning. Get up at 4:00 in the morning and buy his produce . . . and then travel through the east side of Hartford to sell them. And he might have to make one or two trips in the course of the day, pushing that up the hill, the Morgan Street hill, up around the east side, come back, load up again, and do it all over again. And that would take him to maybe 11:00 at night, from 4:00 in the morning to 11:00 at night.

ITALIAN WOMEN'S WORK

Italian tradition kept women from working beside men, so women might work as seamstresses and factory workers with other women. Work in garment factories could be hard. Workers might be required to sit at their machines without breaks. If they were to fall asleep, they would be fired. Often women were not allowed to talk at their machines. Sometimes they were even followed to the restroom "like dogs," according to some immigrant workers. Some women who worked in these factories felt it was like being in prison.

Other common occupations for female Italian immigrants included rolling cigars, making fake flowers, and selling lace. Lace making was a traditional skill that Italian women had handed down through generations since the sixteenth century. Women also rented out rooms to boarders to make extra money. Another job Italian-American women did at home was "piecework," sewing in which they were paid "by the piece." Employers gave them stacks of precut cloth. The women brought these pieces home and sewed them together. For each finished garment, they were paid a certain price. Children often helped them sew garments into the night to earn extra money for the household.

Italian immigrant women's jobs allowed them to work at

Some Italian immigrants found work as pushcart merchants, wheeling their wares through the streets in hopes of making enough sales to earn a day's wage.

home so they could take care of the children. Working was a new concept for Italian women in America. In Italy, there were no jobs for women. When people back in the old country found out about female relatives working, they often did not like the idea.

CHILDREN'S WORK

Boys under 10 took work as bootblacks, who polished rich peoples' shoes. Both boys and girls stood on street corners, selling newspapers. In Pennsylvania, boys worked in coal mines. If they were under age 12, they were supposed to work only above ground. But often, boys would lie and say they were older so that they could work below ground to get better pay. At that time, boys earned anywhere from $1 to $3 per week. Girls

In crowded tenement neighborhoods, many Italian Americans found work in the garment industry. Here, men and women sew neckties on Division Street in New York's "Little Italy." Some Italian women sold lace, rolled cigars, or worked as seamstresses in factories.

who worked were expected to bring home their pay envelopes to their mothers and turn them over unopened. All of their work was to contribute to the family's needs.

WAGES

An Italian immigrant did not necessarily receive fair wages for his or her hard work. There were no laws stipulating equal pay for equal work. In 1906, an Italian ditch digger earned $1.46 for 10 hours of work, while an Irish ditch digger earned $2.00 for the same work. A report by the United State Immigration Commission showed that in 1910 the average Italian-born male earned $396 per year, whereas the national average was $666. Italian immigrants earned even less than African

Americans, who earned an average of $445 in 1910. And Italian women working in garment factories usually earned half of what men made.

One female Italian immigrant recalled working at International Tailoring. Men there made decent wages because there was a union. However, women were not allowed to join the union. "The men used to get swell pay . . . they were getting $45 and $50 in their trade, and I was only getting $18."

Italian Americans still thought they were better off in America than in Italy. They called the United States the land of *dolci dollari* or sweet money. Italian immigrants had a method in America. Often immigrants sent two-thirds of their money back to their family in Italy. If the family was in America, the whole family worked hard, saved money, and took risks. Once they had earned enough money, an immigrant family might open up a small business of their own, perhaps a barbershop or a grocery store or bakery. They could then move from the crowded tenements of New York City to other states where they lived in the Little Italies of Chicago, Boston, San Francisco, and Philadelphia.

5

LIFE IN
A NEW
WORLD

I landed in New York, and when I saw all the buildings I was surprised because I never saw anything like that in my life. I used to see the people pass by me and they were different than the people in the old country. These people that I saw used to walk quiet and they looked like they mind their own business. In Italy when anybody walked on the street they used to whistle and sing. Here they looked like they were mad.

Liberato Dattolo, whose brother sent him money
in 1914 so that he could come to the United States

The millions of immigrants who came to the United States settled mainly in the cities of Boston, New York, Chicago, and Philadelphia. Their neighborhoods were called "Little Italies." Often, one street represented the people of one province

As waves of Italian immigrants arrived in the United States, "Little Italies" began springing up in the major cities. People from the same region in Italy often lived in the same neighborhood (or even the same building) in America—with crowded tenements housing many family members in a single room. Here we see one such neighborhood, on New York's Mulberry Street.

back home in Italy, another street the people of yet another. Sometimes people from one region even settled in the same apartment building. These neighborhoods were urban ghettos. In New York, Italian immigrants lived in lower Manhattan's Mulberry District, or they moved farther north to East Harlem. By 1900, South Philadelphia claimed the second-largest

Italian–American community in the United States. Other Italian immigrant communities included Boston's North End, the near West Side of Chicago ("Little Sicily"), the port area of Baltimore, St. Louis's "Dago Hill," and San Francisco's North Beach.

By the years 1900 to 1920, 340,000 Italians lived in New York City—more than the number of Italians living in the cities of Florence, Venice, and Genoa combined. This meant things were extremely crowded. Families lived in dirty tenements with poor air circulation, little heat, and not enough bathrooms. Running water was a luxury. Tenements were large apartment houses very different from the small single-family homes that Italians were used to. Often, two or three families or even more lived in a one- or two-room tenement unit. This could mean up to 20 people in one apartment with possibly only one cast-iron toilet in the hall on each floor. Because of the crowded, unclean conditions, tuberculosis was fairly common and caused many deaths.

EVERYDAY LIFE IN LITTLE ITALY

Mulberry Street was the heart of Little Italy in New York City. It easily became the center for Italian Americans because it was close to where the Ellis Island ferry dropped off immigrants on the mainland. Before the Italian immigrants came to settle in the Mulberry District, it had been a slum, the kind of place where one did not go after dark. Still a poor place after the Italians came to live there, it was safe and full of life. The area was filled with Italian-owned bakeries, groceries, and produce stores. Empty city lots were turned into small vegetable gardens where Italian tomatoes, parsley, eggplants, and fava beans were grown. Pushcart sellers wandered through the streets selling Italian-imported vegetables such as zucchini and broccoli. Opera music poured from tenement windows, and kitchens were filled with the smells of food and cooking.

One immigrant describes the atmosphere of Hartford, Connecticut's Little Italy where he grew up:

> After the church, I remember them [his grandparents] taking me to the grocery store, to go shopping, because on Sunday they were open, at least half a day. I remember the smells of the Provolone cheese, and all the other imported cheeses from Italy, sausages, salamis, were all hanging in the window. The bakery rushed out—the smell of hot Italian bread, which flowed all over Front Street. It was all over Little Italy, the atmosphere, the sights, the smells, I just loved it. Of course in the Italian supermarkets, I shouldn't say supermarkets—ah, markets—you'd have all kinds of smells of the herbs, Italian herbs and things . . .

In the evenings, women, who now wore colorful clothing and not the black dresses that they wore in Italy, sat on stone stoops (porch steps) or on fire escapes to chat with friends. Men played cards such as *scopa* or turned vacant lots into *bocce* ball courts. Children played in the streets. Barriers were sometimes set up to block traffic to create these play streets. Italian children often played stickball, a game much like baseball, using sewer covers and curbstones for boundaries. Other entertainment popular at the time was live theater. Fare included Neapolitan or Sicilian melodramas, serious contemporary Italian plays, and Sicilian puppet shows. As they had done in their villages back home, Italian immigrants held *festas* (festivals) to celebrate the feast days of saints. In Italian East Harlem, July 16 was the feast of the Madonna of Mt. Carmel, which was celebrated with food, fireworks, music, and a religious procession. Even other ethnic immigrants joined in these festivities.

CRIME IN LITTLE ITALY

There was trouble in these immigrant neighborhoods as well. Thieves considered immigrants easy prey and often used blackmail and violence against them. They insisted on protection

Organized Crime

In the late 1890s, various ethnic gangs became criminal organizations in the United States. These immigrants found criminal activity to be a quick way to economic success. By the 1950s, crime syndicates were no secret and Washington, D.C., authorities began investigating organized crime, connecting Italian Americans to large criminal organizations. Part of a U.S. Senate investigation firmly planted the Mafia concept in the public's mind as a sinister criminal organization run by Italian families. By the 1960s, Americans associated all organized crime with Italians even though other ethnic groups were involved in large crime syndicates, and reports of the Italian underworld took over the country's attention.

Hollywood has helped create a mythology based on the Mafia concept. A series of gangster movies appearing in the 1930s began the popular stereotype of Italians as organized crime figures. Edward G. Robinson portrayed a Brooklyn-raised gangster with an Italian accent in the 1930s film *Little Caesar*. In 1932, actor Paul Muni took on the role of Tony Camonte in *Scarface*. Mafia movies were made in vast numbers after 1945 because they made money at the box office. These films continued to reinforce negative stereotypes of Italian Americans.

One of the most popular Mafia films of all time is *The Godfather*, directed by Francis Ford Coppola. The screenplay was based on Mario Puzo's best-selling 1969 book of the same name. Puzo later admitted that he wrote the book based on accounts he had read in newspapers and never knew a real gangster. In the next five years after the book's publication and success, more than 150 books on the Mafia were released. Italian-American organizations were not happy with the book or the proposed movie, which they believed denigrated the image of Italian Americans. The Italian American Civil Rights League tried to cause trouble for the film. Eventually, the League and the filmmakers compromised. The League would stop causing problems if all references to the Mafia were removed. Because the novel was one of the best sellers in U.S. history, people behind the film felt that not saying the word *Mafia* would fool no one. The film went on to win Academy Awards for best picture, best actor, and best screenplay. Today, with popular television programs like *The Sopranos*, the Mafia stereotype of Italian Americans continues.

money from shopkeepers. If they did not receive this money, the criminals would take action such as harassing the immigrant's customers or breaking store windows. One criminal gang was called the "Black Hand." The following is part of a letter to the *New York Times* by one Italian immigrant haunted by the group:

> . . . At this point the "Black Hand" came into my life and asked me for seven thousand dollars. I told them to go to hell and the bandits tried to blow up my house. Then I asked the police for help and refused more demands, but the Bland Hand set one, two, three, four, five bombs in my houses. Things went to pieces. From 32 tenants I am down to six. I owe a thousand dollars interest that is due next month and I cannot pay. I am a ruined man. My family lives in fear. . . .

By the 1920s, Italian Americans had their own gangs. Other ethnic groups had gangs in ghettos too. These gangs worked to protect the neighborhoods from other immigrant groups.

ORGANIZATIONS

Italian Americans also started their own mutual aid societies, clubs, and associations. Through these organizations members could buy life insurance and get hospital care for members by paying dues of $0.30 to $0.60 each month. Members of these places often had common roots back home in the same Italian village or province. The clubhouses of these associations became meeting places for athletic teams and social events. One of the best known of these organizations is the Order of the Sons of Italy founded by Dr. Vincenzo Sellaro in 1905. It became a national organization with 1,300 branches, and its members today are successful business leaders, lawyers, and doctors.

Italian-language publications were extremely popular in immigrant neighborhoods. They often were the inspiration for discussions and debates throughout the neighborhood about current events and issues. The first Italian-language newspaper in the United States was a weekly, *L'Eco d'Italia,* which began publication in 1849. New York City was home to the first Italian-American daily newspaper published in the Italian language, *Il Progresso Italo-Americano.* In this newspaper, immigrants could find news of events happening back in Italy. *Il Progresso,* still published today, grew to be the largest and most influential of the Italian-American newspapers. Generoso Pope, who had started out a poor immigrant from the province of Benevento, owned the newspaper and, because of its success, became one of the first Italian–American millionaires. His son, Generoso Pope, Jr., went on to publish the *National Enquirer.*

WOMEN'S LIFE

The women, unfamiliar with tenement living, taught each other how to cook on tenement stoves and shared home remedies from the old country. When they shopped, they bargained over prices, trying to get the best deal. They also looked out for each other's children.

Italian immigrant women imported Old World rituals and remedies. For example, they might have their children wear camphor balls or garlic to ward off polio. Superstition might lead them to believe that someone put the "evil eye" on one of their children, and that was why the child had a headache. To get rid of the headache, the Italian mother might drop oil in water while praying and then rub the water and oil on the child's forehead.

RELIGION

In America, religion remained as important as Old World superstition to the Italian immigrants. Religion kept them connected to the old country. Most immigrants were Roman Catholic and found the church to be a source of strength. However, upon arrival in America, Italian immigrants discovered that Irish Americans controlled the Catholic Church, and

Wherever Italian immigrants settled, they brought their rich customs and traditions with them. Since each Italian town had its own patron saint, it was only natural that Italians living in the same neighborhood in America would celebrate that saint's feast day with food, games, and parades.

their religious customs and traditions were very different from those of the Italians.

Over the centuries, the peasants of Italy had developed their own religious practices, which included patron saints of villages. They built shrines to these saints in their fields and homes and celebrated feast days with processions through the village. Italian Catholics became freer in their worship. Veneration of the Virgin Mary and different saints was central to their religion. Italian Catholics named their children after saints and prayed to the saints. The Italian immigrants of the 1880s to the 1920s treated local priests and saints like members of the family. Many Italian immigrants also brought anticlericalism with them to the United States. They felt hostility to the clergy because the pope had been Italy's largest landholder and had stood in the way of Italian unification.

The Irish clergy had a stricter view of worship. Irish Catholics were more pious and more observant of doctrine. For example, most went to church regularly every Sunday. Because of these differences, Italian immigrants were often denied access to the church. If they were allowed in, they were allowed to worship only in the church's basement. Italian immigrants also felt that they did not want to "pay to pray" and did not like the focus on donating money to the church in America. By the 1920s, Italian Americans began to build many of their own churches, which they often named after saints revered in Italy. One of the first Italian churches meant specifically for new immigrants was the Church of Our Lady of Loreto, which opened in 1892 on Elizabeth Street in New York. Italian immigrants also held their festas. These summer feasts in honor of the saints were yet another way of connecting to the old country and included a procession of people singing and carrying candles while walking barefoot to show their faith. Two festivals—Mulberry Street's Neapolitan Feast of San Gennaro and Astoria's Feast of the Lilies—are still celebrated.

Perhaps the barrier between Irish Catholics and Italian Catholics was finally broken down in 1982. That was the year Archbishop Joseph Bernardin of Chicago, the son of an immigrant stone carver, became the first Italian–American cardinal of the Catholic Church.

DISCRIMINATION AGAINST ITALIANS

Religious discrimination was not the only discrimination that Italian immigrants faced. Prejudice in America was similar to the political oppression they had faced in Italy. Italian immigrants were stereotyped as people who were involved in crime and willing to kill for passion or revenge; people who were violent, emotional, and unable to control themselves in public; people who did not want to mix; and people who did not want to be American. The stereotyped image of docile and ignorant Italian immigrants was common and was perpetuated by vaudeville comics, writers, and cartoonists. It was shameful to be Italian, and many areas of the United States considered Italians to be non-white. Italians were thought to have a strange language, culture, and religion, as well as strange customs and superstitions.

Italian immigrants were laughed at for the way they dressed and talked, discriminated against because of their darker skin, different religion, customs, and language, and because of their occupations. On trains, they were denied access to sleeping and dining cars. Porters and brakemen refused to assist Italian immigrant women with children and baggage. Train crews did not help Italian immigrants disembark at the right stations; yet these immigrants paid the same fare as everyone else. Perhaps worst of all, agents separated families and put them on different trains arriving at stations at various times.

Italian immigrants were called derogatory names such as WOP, Dago, or Wiole. The term *wop* came from "without passport," which was stamped by immigration officials on entry papers of the people who came to America and had left Italy without applying for official permission to leave their country. It is uncertain where the term dago originated. Possibly, it applied to Italian immigrants who worked day labor jobs, meaning "day-go."

Second-generation Italians were especially hurt by prejudice because they lived between two worlds. Fiorello La Guardia, who became mayor of New York City, told about how he was taunted as a child in Arizona where his father was stationed at an army post. When an Italian organ grinder came, La Guardia was teased by the other children and called a dago. After La Guardia became mayor of New York, he banned organ grinders from the city's streets.

FAMILY VALUES

The Italians' protection against these prejudices was the family, the root of Italian tradition. Keeping children, parents, and grandparents together was important. It was *La Via Vecchia*,

Italian immigrants did not always feel welcome in their adopted homeland. Anti-Italian prejudice was widespread, as reflected in this racist cartoon that suggests "gifts" of an organ grinder, shoeshine box, and basket of apples for newly arrived immigrants.

which meant the old ways. In the United States as in Italy, the family remained the strongest social unit. The father was the head of the family, and the mother was the center. The father's job included providing for the wife and children, protecting them, and making decisions regarding their welfare. For his hard work, at the end of the working day, he was to be greeted with a ready and hearty meal. The mother's duties included handling the finances, controlling the children's behavior, arranging marriages, and taking care of social obligations. She was the source of the family's warmth and security.

She might spend hours on a meal to show her devotion to her family. Any conflict in the family or a child's misbehavior reflected on her within the community.

CLASH OF OLD AND NEW VALUES

In America, the old ways began clashing with the new ways. Parents were trying to keep their traditions and customs, and they did not like what they saw as "American ways." They had good intentions; they came to America in the first place because they wanted their children's lives to be better.

Italian immigrants found it hard to pass on their values to their children because American values of marriage and family were much different. An example of an Italian value is that young women were not supposed to go out of the house alone. They needed to have a chaperone. Sons, however, were given more freedom in America. This situation caused conflict within the family because the girl often thought, "If I'm going out to work, why shouldn't I be able to go out at other times too?"

Some children did go to school in America. Attending American schools helped children adapt more quickly than parents to living in America. Italian boys, for example, might help their fathers read forms. One scholar and historian, however, was forbidden to speak English at home because his parents were afraid of losing that very important communication with their own children. One second-generation Italian said that as a young child, the Italian-language radio station WOV was regularly played in his household. So naturally, he believed growing up in Little Italy that he actually lived in Italy. On his first day of school, he did not say "good morning" to the teacher but rather "Buon Giorno." He was almost immediately sent to a special class to learn English. Some parents believed that children with more education would separate from the family, so they did not encourage their children to attend school.

The second generation of Italian Americans was basically living in two worlds. They were Italian at home and American everywhere else. Sometimes in public they would find themselves embarrassed by the behavior and language of their elders. For the most part, the first generation spoke Italian better than English, ate only Italian food, and desired only Italian friends. The second generation, however, spoke English on the street, at school, and at work, and Italian at home. The second generation was both American and Italian in its customs. At school, second-generation Italian Americans were looked down on not only by fellow students but also by teachers. Sometimes this made children resent their own parents.

Back in Sicily, fathers could expect obedience from each family member, as is evident in this statement by an immigrant father of 10:

> My children have been brought up my way and the Italian way. This I mean is that the children should always ask the father when they want to do something that they are not sure of. In Italy I was taught that what my father said was right. I have done this with my children and they have to do it; if they don't they can't live in my house. What I say is the law in my house. . . .

In America, fathers found they were losing that power. Children, once they reached the legal age, could do as they pleased. Italian-American children were no longer okay with arranged marriages and having their father choose where they would work. They began to go to college, and girls who had once been expected to marry and have children instead decided to go on to college and have careers.

PREJUDICE TURNS UGLY

Prejudice took an especially ugly turn in many cases. Two of the most notorious were the Louisiana lynchings of 1890 and the Sacco and Vanzetti murder trial.

In Louisiana, by the late 1800s, the French Quarter of New Orleans had become known as "Little Palermo" because it was filled mostly with merchants and restaurateurs from Sicily.

Racial tension filled the city as well. By the 1890s, bigotry in New Orleans was increasing. Sicilians had been coming to New Orleans since the Civil War and had success in fishing and importing fruits. However, a growing population of Sicilian fishermen was seen as taking work from the Irish. As a result, newspapers featured unflattering cartoons depicting Italians as dirty, illiterate, lazy, and dangerous people.

Then one event cost the lives of several Italian Americans. On October 15, 1890, a rainy New Orleans night, Police Chief David Hennessy was gunned down. Before he died, he supposedly said that "the dagos" did it, referring to Italian-American day laborers. At the time, however, many New Orleans police and city officials were corrupt and were probably suspects themselves. Police rounded up 300 Italian-American men, and, of these, nine stood trial. A jury found all nine not guilty.

A mob of angry citizens disagreed, however, and dragged the men into the streets along with two other Italian immigrants not even connected to the case. Among the lynch mob were "respectable" doctors and lawyers. They tied ropes to a tree and hung two Italian Americans that night. They shot and killed nine others. It was the largest lynching in United States history.

The killings brought official protest from the Italian government, and there was even talk of war over the incident. However, the talk died down, and nothing ever came of it. To this day, no one knows who really shot Police Chief Hennessy, but the incident stirred a hatred that lasted for years. During the 1890s, at least 22 Italian Americans were lynched in the United States, including the 11 in New Orleans.

On April 15, 1920, a paymaster and guard were killed in a robbery at a shoe factory in Braintree, Massachusetts. Nicola Sacco and Bartolomeo Vanzetti were arrested for the crime. The two naturalized Italian immigrant men spoke little English. Sacco worked in a shoe factory. Vanzetti was a fish peddler. However, both men held anarchist views.

Most people believe that Sacco and Vanzetti were not really

Nicola Sacco (left) and Bartolomeo Vanzetti (center) were two Italian immigrants whose anarchist views worked against them. Arrested for murder and robbery committed in Massachusetts, both received a less-than-fair trial and were sentenced to death.

tried for murder but that the basic right of freedom of speech was being challenged in their trial. In Boston, people protested that the two men were not being tried for murder but for their political views. For Italian Americans, the case was not about murder; it was about being different in American society.

Sacco and Vanzetti did not receive a fair trial. The judge presiding over their trial was openly hostile to Italians. Being Italian immigrants and anarchists was enough to find the two men guilty. The verdict sent a message to Italian Americans that they were not wanted in the United States.

Six years and several attempts by a lawyer to appeal the case to a higher court went by with no success. Still maintaining their innocence, both men died in the electric chair on August 27, 1927, and there was widespread protest in both the United States and Europe. Before his death sentence was carried out Vanzetti said, "I am suffering because I am a radical and indeed I am a radical; I have suffered because I was an Italian, and indeed I am an Italian . . . I have finished. Thank you."

IMMIGRATION RESTRICTIONS

Around this time, the United States government started to change immigration laws. Between 1880 and 1930, more than 27 million people had entered the United States, and about 20 million of those had come through Ellis Island. With the start of World War I in 1914, American attitudes had begun to change regarding immigration. Nationalism was on the rise, and so were people's suspicions of foreigners.

In 1921, a temporary law limited the number of immigrants allowed into the nation. Three years later in 1924, immigration laws were revised completely. The new laws set a limit of 150,000 European immigrants each year. Each country had a quota equal to 2 percent of its population in the United States as of 1890. These new laws gave preference to immigrants that had arrived earlier in the United States and restricted later immigrants. For example, this meant that immigrants could still come from Nordic states, meaning blonde, blue-eyed, fair-haired immigrants would be allowed in greater numbers. However, the 1924 immigration laws kept most eastern and southern Europeans from entering the United States, and that included Italians and Jews. However, the Italian immigrants already here and those who continued to filter in made their mark on America.

6

THE "DAGOES" RISE UP

Factories, mines, and mills were part of what paved the way to the future for Italian men, women, and children as they filled a major part of the labor force. Italian–American workers stood up against big business and labor abuses. Anthony Tapogna emigrated with his family from Italy at age 10 in 1920 and later became a successful lawyer:

> At least the opportunity was here to develop, to enlarge, to have available an opportunity somewhere in the distance—still out of reach, but maybe we could reach it, as was my good fortune. By hard work to be able to reach an opportunity that I never would have had in Italy. I was born a farmer's son; I would have died a farmer. Like the rest of us. There wouldn't have been a chance to go to school, or an occasion to go into a profession. It

In the coal mines of Pennsylvania, it was not uncommon to see child laborers like these. Soon, Italian Americans began to play a major role in the unions that reformed workplace safety standards and expanded workers' rights.

was only my friend, who is a doctor there now, whose father was the padrone; he was the owner of that town and of wealth and that's why he's a doctor today. I wouldn't have had that opportunity. No, indeed.

The Italians' involvement in unions and organized strike action occurred basically from the beginning in all areas of American industry. They became active in radical union organizations such as the Industrial Workers of the World (IWW). A small number were anarchists (people that oppose any type of government).

Italians fought back and became leaders of labor unions. They fought for better wages and better working conditions. Italian Americans led mine workers in strikes in the West. They led silk workers in strikes in New Jersey. In a major turn of events for the labor movement, they also led textile workers in a strike in New England.

MINING

To industrialize the nation, mining was a necessity. Mines were located in isolated areas such as Minnesota, Utah, Idaho, and Colorado. Mining towns were usually run by managers who worked for owners who lived offsite in big cities such as New York or San Francisco. Mining was low-paying work, especially considering the dangers it involved. Death by accidents in mines was high. In Colorado alone in 1910, 323 miners were killed in mines. One particularly terrible accident occurred at the St. Paul Mine Company in Cherry, Illinois, in November 1909. While 500 men were working in the mines, a wagon full of hay going down to feed the mules below ground caught fire. The hay fire was put out, but nearby timbers began to burn and went unnoticed. After the fire was spotted, the ventilation system was shut down to cut off the oxygen supply to the fire. The miners could not breathe. The ventilation system was turned back on and the blaze burned out of control. In all, 250 men died; 73 were Italians.

Because of the low pay, many miners were forced to work two jobs just to keep food on the table for their families. Company stores, which sold goods to the miners of mining towns, charged exorbitant rates—often 100 percent more than other business did for the same goods. However, miners did not have easy access to any place other than the company store. Working equipment was not provided for the miners and had to be rented, thus incorporating another expense. Shovels, pick-axes, and carts all had to be rented by the miners themselves. If miners complained about any of these working conditions, the local militia could be called in to settle the matter. In other words, workers had little say and few rights.

Life in these mining towns was not easy, as this immigrant's story shows:

> Since the homes were all owned by the company, you had to accommodate all the coal miners who arrived, they would require you to feed and board for a small fee. These homes had no basements, linoleum was unknown then, to keep the home livable it required getting down on your hands and knees and scrub the boards clean.
>
> My mom was required to cook and bake on a coal stove. Light was obtained by a kerosene lamp. Heat in the house was given by a round coal stove. Coal had to be hauled on your back from the coal mine, which was situated about two miles from your home. Flour was bought in 100 lb. bags, nothing was discarded, my mom would bleach out the name of the flour company and make us undergarments, towels, etc. . . .

LUDLOW MASSACRE

At Coeur d'Alene, Idaho, striking miners clashed with militia and strikebreakers, resulting in 100 wounded miners. However, of all mining confrontations between miners and owners, the most devastating occurred on April 20, 1914, in a strike by the United Mine Workers against John D. Rockefeller, Jr.'s Colorado Fuel and Iron Company Works. Participating in this strike were mainly English and Italian immigrants along with some Greeks, Slavs, Austrians, and Mexicans. They were fighting for union recognition, increased wages, an 8-hour workday, and the right to trade in other than company-owned stores. During the strike, the strikers and their families (a total of about 1,000 people) lived in tents near the Ludlow coal mines. One day,

A 1914 strike by United Mine Workers in Colorado resulted in violence. Strikebreakers and government troops fired guns at the tents where the strikers and their families lived, starting a fire that killed 45, including two Italian women and ten children.

troops fired machine guns at the tent colony—consisting of mainly women and children—and the canvas tents ignited. At least 45 people died in the flames, including two Italian women and ten children. A military investigation into the incident showed that the troops, with the assistance of strikebreakers, deliberately started the fire, with the intention of destroying the entire colony and everyone in it. An open war in the state followed the event and lasted for eight days. The incident became known as the Ludlow Massacre.

RADICAL UNIONS

Italians, because they were considered unskilled workers, were not allowed in established unions. For this reason, Italian immigrants gravitated toward radical unions, such as the IWW. One such established union was the American Federation of Labor. By imposing special requirements, the organization made it virtually impossible for Italian immigrants to join the union. One special requirement was an initiation fee of $500. For most immigrants, this was one year's wages. By joining other more radical unions, immigrants could run the risk of being shot, lynched, or deported.

In 1908, in Tampa, Florida, Italian immigrants made up 20 percent of the cigar industry labor force. While the immigrants worked, they listened to a reader of their choosing or *El lector*. The reader read materials in four shifts as encouraged by the company: national news, international politics, news from the industrial world, and excerpts from novel such as Victor Hugo's *Les Misérables* and Cervantes' *Don Quixote*. From these readings, some workers were inspired to join radical unions. After strikes and clashes, the company replaced the reader with the radio.

RECRUITING FROM OVERSEAS

In some instances, workers were recruited overseas. In 1885, the U.S. Congress enacted contract labor laws, making it illegal to recruit foreign workers before they reached the United States. It was easy to get around these laws, though, and recruiters still went to Italy promising workers steady employment, decent pay, and good housing. When the men recruited by these agents arrived in America, their experience was much different. They often found themselves stripped of their money and abandoned in an unfamiliar land. Sometimes employment agencies encouraged employers to fire workers so the agencies could replace them with a new crew. In such instances, the agency would share the new employment fees with the employers. After being hired by one such recruiting agent, an Italian immigrant recalled, "Our daily fare was coffee and bread for breakfast, rice with lard or soup at dinnertime, and cheese or sausage for supper. Yet we were not able to pay off our debt; so after a while we were given only bread. . . . "

Textile mills also tried their hand at recruiting immigrants from overseas. The American Woolen Company initiated a recruiting campaign around the year 1900. Throughout Europe, the company hung poster ads showing happy workers living in homes with picket fences. They also showed men and women reading while holding onto bags of gold. But the reality in America for the workers of American Woolen Company were crowded stone tenements with rents so high that families had to share living quarters. Salaries were so low that entire families—fathers, mothers, and children—had to work 56 hours a week. Men earned $9 a week, whereas women and children earned less for the exact same work.

STRIKE AGAINST TEXTILE INDUSTRY

Italian labor leaders Arturo Giovannitti and Guiseppe Ettor led an important strike in 1912 in a Lawrence, Massachusetts, textile factory. Although many strikes had occurred before, this was the turning point for American labor unions. In 1912, Lawrence, Massachusetts produced more cloth than any other city in the world. The city's textile mills had 50,000 men, women, and children working in them—many Italian immigrants. The strike was instigated when the Massachusetts legislature recognized the poor conditions of the textile factory and passed a law reducing the work week for women and children from 56 to 54 hours per week. The legislature's move angered the textile factory owners who decided to in turn cut the salaries of women and children by $0.32, at a time when bread cost $0.10 a loaf. Other conditions at the mill had the workers upset as well. If children were late three times, they were fired. Bosses told women that to keep their jobs they would have to engage in sexual relations with them. Supervisors called workers "ignorant Dagoes."

Workers did not discover the pay loss until the day they opened their pay envelopes. Almost immediately, they began shouting and smashing the factory machinery. They blew fuses and fled to the streets yelling, "Better to starve fighting than to starve working." In a matter of days, 20,000 workers had joined the strike. The union at the time had only 3,000 members. The IWW had only 300.

The local IWW chapter asked the New York IWW to send help. Assistance came in the form of two men, Arturo Giovannitti, age 27, and Guiseppe Ettor, age 26. Both men could speak English and Italian fluently. During the strike, Ettor made certain that interpreters were available for each ethnic group participating in the strike. With these interpreters, he encouraged workers of all backgrounds—Poles, Italians, Germans, French, Lithuanians, Portuguese, and Syrians—to stick with the strike regardless of the hardship. He also organized committees with elected representatives of men and women from each mill. Giovannitti took it upon himself to set up soup kitchens and distribute food to the striking workers and their families.

Italian Americans and other ethnic group workers faced local militiamen armed with bayonets. Massachusetts so desperately wanted the strike to end that it offered credit on mid-term exams for Harvard University students who would serve in the Lawrence militia. Many strikers were arrested, including three who were given prison sentences of two years by a judge who said, "the only way to teach them is to deal out the severest sentences." Eventually, after one clash, even Ettor and Giovannitti were charged with murder and jailed.

Giovannitti's soup kitchens were not holding out, and the striking workers were hungry. They began to send their children to family members around the nation. Thousands left, and the story made national headlines. Americans were heartbroken at the sight of these half-starved children. The mill owners did not like the negative publicity and did not want any more children to leave town. Fifty police and two groups of state militia came to the train station, clubbing children and beating the mothers who were trying to protect them. In the end, 300 people were arrested, and one person was killed in the clash. The women and children were thrown into trucks while reporters watched.

The scene prompted a congressional investigation into working conditions at the mill. Once the U.S. government became involved, it found that the mill indeed was negligent. During testimony by mill workers, one teenager described how her scalp had been ripped off when her hair had been caught in a loom. Others told of having to buy false birth certificates to work because they were not yet 14 years old. The teenagers' other stories included losing an hour's pay for being two minutes late and not receiving any pay for overtime. The mill owners' first offer was a 5 percent pay increase. However, after negotiations, the workers received an offer of a 15 percent increase, time and a quarter for overtime, and the promise of no reprisals for the strikers. More important, the strikers brought the poor working conditions of factory workers into the open. The incident strengthened labor unions across the United States.

CHANGING POLITICAL SCENE

Two years after the Lawrence, Massachusetts, strike, World War I began. The song "Over There" was an extremely popular war anthem (song of praise or celebration) that reflected American patriotism. It was sung by Italian–American Opera singer Enrico Caruso and symbolized Italian–American patriotism. Caruso's concerts earned millions of dollars for the Allied Forces, and by 1914, Caruso was the first recording artist to sell 1 million records.

However, even Caruso's popularity could not stop the bigotry against Italian Americans influenced by the war. Because of the war, people suspected of being radicals were looked at closely by the government. Because of involvement in the labor movement, this included many Italian Americans.

FIORELLO LA GUARDIA

By the 1920s, Italians were moving more toward the Democratic clubs in New York, and in the 1930s a small number of Italian Americans broke into Irish-controlled New York City politics. Salvatore Cotillo, a young attorney from East Harlem, was the first Italian to be elected to the New York State Assembly. One of the first Italian Americans to really achieve success in American politics was Fiorello La Guardia. La Guardia was born in New York in Little Italy on December 11, 1882. His father was from Foggia, Italy. His mother came from Trieste (then a part of Austria, but today an Italian city) and was Jewish. His father was an accomplished musician who had come to America in 1878. Because his father was a band conductor for the U.S. Army, La Guardia's family traveled a lot, but Fiorello spent most of his childhood in Arizona. As a young man, he lived in Greenwich Village where he was acquainted with Arturo Giovannitti, the poet and labor leader. He also worked as a file clerk at the American consulate in Budapest, Hungary. In his extra time, La Guardia learned German, French, and Yiddish and mastered Italian.

When he returned to New York, La Guardia graduated from law school and began representing labor unions. His first run for a congressional seat in the House of Representatives ended in failure. However, two years later, in 1916, he won a

Among the first Italian Americans to achieve a position of prominence was Fiorello La Guardia. The son of Italian immigrants, La Guardia was born in New York's "Little Italy" and eventually became mayor of the city. Today, a major New York City airport still bears his name.

congressional seat despite political corruption at the time. He soon resigned from Congress, however, to join the U.S. Air Service on the Austrian–Italian front in 1917. He served first as lieutenant, then as captain, and finally as major. In 1921, he returned to politics and vied for the Republican nomination for

Notable Italian–American Men

Al Capone (1899–1947) Capone was born in 1899 in Naples and came to America as a child. He grew up in Brooklyn, New York, but went to Chicago after a fight. He brought together gangs of Irish, Polish, and African Americans. In the 1920s and 1930s, under one management, these gangs became a mighty force, and Capone became known in the popular press as "Public Enemy Number One." Capone never belonged to a nationwide Mafia, but his exploits added to the Mafia myth. In 1931, he was convicted of tax evasion and sent to Alcatraz prison.

Joseph Barbera (1911–) The man behind *Tom and Jerry, Yogi Bear, The Flintstones, The Jetsons, The Smurfs,* and *Scooby-Doo* was born in New York City in 1911. He met William Hanna at MGM studios in 1937. The men collaborated to create many cartoon characters. Their *Tom and Jerry* cartoons won seven best-animated short film Oscars, and Barbera also received eight Emmy awards, a star on the Hollywood Walk of Fame, and many other honors.

Joe DiMaggio (1914–1999) DiMaggio, the son of a Sicilian immigrant father, was born in Martinez, California, on November 25, 1914. In 1936, DiMaggio joined the New York Yankees. He had a 56-game hitting streak in 1941, the longest in history. In 1954, he married Marilyn Monroe. DiMaggio was voted American League Most Valuable Player three times during his 13 seasons with the Yankees. In 1950, DiMaggio was voted baseball's "Greatest Living Player." In 1955, he was inducted into the Baseball Hall of Fame. He died March 8, 1999 at age 84.

Antonin Scalia (1936–) The first Italian-American Supreme Court Justice was born on March 11, 1936 in Trenton, New Jersey. Scalia graduated magna cum laude from Harvard Law School. After teaching law at the University of Virginia, Scalia left to work for various government and law-related posts for Presidents Nixon, Carter, and Reagan. In 1986, Reagan appointed Scalia to the U.S. Supreme Court.

Rudolph W. Giuliani (1944–) Giuliani was born in 1944, first attending Manhattan College, then law school. He began his career in the U.S attorney's office for the Southern District of New York. From 1968 to 1992, working for the U.S. Department of Justice, he cracked down on drug traffickers and organized crime. In 1993, he was elected mayor of New York City and re-elected in 1997. Under Giuliani, crime in New York City diminished 41 percent. *Time* magazine named him Man of the Year in 2001 for holding the City of New York together after the terrorist attacks of September 11, 2001.

mayor of New York City, which he lost. A Republican political boss confided in La Guardia that New York was not ready for an Italian-American mayor.

After this disappointment, La Guardia made a successful 10-year return to the House of Representatives, where he spoke out for workers' rights such as a minimum wage, hourly work limits, and elimination of child labor. In 1924, he fought against the discriminatory immigration laws.

In 1933, La Guardia again made a run for New York City mayor—this time successfully. From 1934 to 1945, he served three consecutive terms, endearing himself to many in the City of New York. He became known as "Little Flower," a translation of his first name. As mayor, La Guardia made his mark on history by fighting against the city's political corruption and implementing programs to clear the city of slums and creating projects to beautify the city. He was an expert at using drama to gain support for his causes. He rode to fires on fire engines and with sledge-hammers smashed slot machines that his government declared illegal. La Guardia worked hard as mayor, often putting in 16-hour days. He was known and respected for his honesty. In 1945, La Guardia chose not to run for re-election. Instead, after his retirement, he became director of the United Nations Relief and Rehabilitation Administration, where he worked for the relief of wartime refugees. He died in 1947.

WORLD WAR II MAKES ENEMIES OF ITALIAN AMERICANS

World War II was the turning point for Italian Americans in the United States, a time when many finally started to blend into American society. When the war first began, many Italian Americans admired Benito Mussolini, Italy's dictator. He had brought prosperity to their poor land and had finally settled the long dispute with the Catholic Church. In fact, much of the world admired the man for having turned Italy—the Old Country—into a modern nation. Even President Roosevelt sent several of his staff members to Italy to learn from Mussolini's social programs, which included government sponsorship of the arts and support for social security. However, Mussolini fell out of favor with many nations when he invaded Ethiopia in 1935. Because of his action, the League of Nations imposed economic sanctions against Italy. Seeing this as betrayal, many Italian Americans did what they could to support the land where they still had relatives. To aid the Italian war effort, some people made donations to the Italian Red Cross. Thousands of other Italian Americans sent their gold wedding rings or copper postcards.

Then in 1936, Mussolini allied himself with Nazi Germany, and in June 1940, Italy joined Germany in the invasion of France. At this action, President Roosevelt called Mussolini a "jackal" who had lunged a "dagger" into the "back of his neighbor." With these words, Italian Americans feared that they would soon be at war with their homeland. On December 7, 1941, Japan attacked Pearl Harbor, and as a result the United States could no longer ignore the war taking place elsewhere in the world. It declared war on Japan, Germany, and Italy.

When the United States declared war on Italy, most Italian Americans became tense, afraid of how they would be treated by the American government. During World War I, the situation had been much different. Italy had been on the side of the United States; now it was the enemy. Italian immigrants loved both countries, and having to choose sides struck at the heart of the Italian-American community. Many Italian immigrants in the United States at this time were not yet citizens. In fact, many Italian immigrants did not want to become U.S. citizens because they believed that they would someday return to Italy. It also took much effort for uneducated persons to become citizens because passing a literacy exam was required. The repeated migration of these "birds of passage" caused animosity, and Italian immigrants were accused of being un-American. Italian immigrants began to believe that acceptance would come as soon as they became U.S. citizens. Unfortunately, this did not prove true in industrial cities where jobs were getting hard to compete for.

In the end, Italians Americans chose to fight for their country—the United States. Millions showed their patriotism by staging rallies and supporting Red Cross efforts. Many Italian-American men volunteered, and many were drafted. In fact, more than 500,000 Italian–American men served in the armed forces during World War II.

Regardless of this support, Italian immigrants were still under suspicion. The American government placed 600,000 Italian immigrants without citizenship in America on an enemy alien list along with thousands of other non-citizens living in the United States. Italian aliens became enemy aliens. In January 1942, all enemy aliens were required to register at their local post office. They had to be fingerprinted and photographed, and they were required to carry their photo identification "enemy alien registration cards" at all times. Some of the restrictions placed on enemy aliens and sometimes even on naturalized citizens included:

- Travel: no travel beyond a five-mile radius of home; longer trips required application for travel permit.
- Contraband: all firearms, short-wave radios, cameras, and "signaling devices" (including flashlights) were prohibited; all were to be turned in or confiscated (most were never returned).
- Curfew: enemy aliens on the West Coast were confined to their homes between 8 P.M. and 6 A.M.

These restrictions ended up creating employment and food-supply problems that the government did not count on.

During World War II, Italian Americans were regarded with suspicion. Deemed "enemy aliens," all were forced to register with the government at their local post office, and hundreds were sent to internment camps like this one in Missoula, Montana. The internment of Italian, Japanese, and German Americans during the war was a dark moment in America's history

IMPRISONMENT AND RELOCATION

Two-hundred-fifty more Italian immigrants were forced into internment camps in Montana, Oklahoma, Tennessee, and Texas. The number of those interned (confined) rose to 1,521 by June 1942, many for curfew violations alone. The procedure for arrest and internment was not a pleasant one. FBI officers arrived at a family or individual's home at night. They searched the home, then took the individual to an Immigration Service detention facility. The family was never told why the arrest was being made or what would happen to their loved one. Most arrestees were later sent by train to Fort Missoula, Montana. There they were given hearings before boards made up of military officers and lay people. The arrestees were not informed of the charges against them nor were they given legal counsel.

Even more immigrants were forced to relocate away from the coasts, which were considered sensitive areas. Catherine Buccellato was one Italian immigrant forced to leave her Pittsburg, California, home during the war. Ironically, her son, Nick, was off fighting the war. When he came home on leave, he found the house empty. Also in Pittsburg, housing was so hard to find that Bettina Troia had to live in a chicken coop during her evacuation.

Some people tried to hold on to their jobs during the evacuation. William Ardente was labeled an enemy alien in 1942. When he tried to keep his job, he was told to drop the "e" from the end of his name to Americanize it. He did so, but lost his job anyway. During this time, women were also in a desperate situation because of the Cable Act of 1916. Under the terms of this act, even American-born women lost their citizenship if they married an Italian man. Elaine Null, who worked as a postal employee, had to fingerprint her own mother as an enemy alien for this reason.

In October 1942, Italian immigrants were released from the relocation program. They were the only group taken off the list during the war. At the time, they were considered not to be as dangerous as the Germans and Japanese.

MOVE TO THE SUBURBS

After the Great Depression, businesses in Little Italies were not doing well, and many Italians Americans were out of work. Still, the prosperity that occurred in the nation after World War II helped the economic status of Italian Americans. Many families moved from Little Italies to the suburbs. This move took them away from stereotypes but also from their traditions. Many Italian Americans now wanted to become "Americanized" and began hiding their Italian identity.

7 INTO THE MELTING POT:
The Italian–American Influence

> Well, to be an Italian American—I'm very proud of it, because it's being part of a wonderful tradition, a wonderful tradition of people who came to this country with nothing . . . nothing and built themselves up to be what we are today.
>
> **—Chazz Palminteri, actor/writer/director**

Italian Americans worked hard, saved their money, and eventually moved from the Little Italies of America to the suburbs. Italian Americans who had served in World War II were eligible for assistance from the G.I. Bill. About 1 million Italian Americans served in the armed forces, and the G.I. Bill provided these people with money for college tuition and loans for homes and small businesses. Many Italian–American veterans took advantage of these opportunities. Some started construction

One of the twentieth century's most famous Italian Americans was the singer and actor, Frank Sinatra. Born the son of Italian immigrants in Hoboken, New Jersey, Sinatra became famous worldwide and enjoyed a long and celebrated career in music and film.

businesses that did well because of the home building boom after the war. Some, such as Lee Iacocca, the head of Chrysler Corporation, went to college and became skilled business leaders. Others became doctors, lawyers, poets, novelists, teachers, and movie directors.

Francesco Alberto Sinatra, a second-generation Italian American, was born to Sicilian parents in 1915. Also known as

Frank Sinatra, the young boy grew up in Hoboken, New Jersey, where his father was a fireman and his mother did work for a local politician. Because of their jobs, Sinatra had a better life than did most Italian immigrant children who grew up during the Depression. However, it was not without its share of heartache. Sinatra often said, "I'll never forget how it hurt when kids called me a 'dago' when I was a boy."

His interest in music started early. As a boy, Sinatra was given a ukulele by one of his uncles. As a teenager, he sang in small nightclubs, at church dances, and in local bars. As an adult, Sinatra became a wildly popular singer and early in his career was called "the voice of American music." His other nicknames included simply "The Voice" and "Chairman of the Board." During his 60-year career, Sinatra made more than 2,000 recordings, various movies, and numerous television and cabaret appearances. Sinatra was an Oscar, Emmy, and Grammy-winning legend. In an unprecedented move, he used his celebrity status in 1945 to film public service announcements promoting racial tolerance. He also raised millions of dollars for charities. Suggestions that he was tied to organized crime angered Sinatra. He often said, "If I get together with two other Italians it's called mafia." Leaving a legacy of well-remembered tunes and films, Sinatra died in 1998.

In the 1950s, Sinatra's crooning inspired a great line of successful Italian-American singers who made American songs popular around the world: Dino Crocetti (Dean Martin), Pierino (Perry) Como, Giuliano (Julius) La Rosa, Antonio Benedetto (Tony Bennett), Vito Farinola (Vic Damone), Annette Funicello, Concetta Franconero (Connie Francis), Walden Cassotto (Bobby Darin), Frank Lo Vecchio (Frankie Laine), and Sal Mineo. Sinatra's success even inspired singer Tony Martin who pretended to be of Italian heritage. These singers all brought much-needed happiness to the country in the decades after the Depression and the end of World War II.

Italian Americans may have had meager beginnings, but they made a point to save their money earned from all their hard work. They eventually moved up from pick-and-shovel jobs and left the streets as organ grinders and pushcart peddlers to open their own businesses. These Italian-run grocery stores, restaurants, and other businesses opened in immigrant neighborhoods, and some became real success stories.

SUCCESS STORIES

One such success story is that of Amadeo Obici, who left Italy to go to Scranton, Ohio, where he worked at his uncle's fruit stand. Obici learned English as he worked. By saving his money, he was able to start his own business in 1897. He rented sidewalk space and sold a paper bags full of roasted peanuts for $0.05 each. Obici came up with an ingenious idea. In each bag, he placed a coupon with one letter of his name on it. If a customer collected all the letters to spell Obici's full name, the customer received a pocket watch. The gimmick worked, and the Planters Peanut Company had begun. By 1930, the company had four huge plants, and made more than $12 million annually. Some people called Obici "The Peanut King."

Around the year 1915, Ettore (Hector) Boiardi began as a chef's apprentice at age 11. When he came to America, Boiardi worked as a hotel chef; moving from hotel to hotel, his reputation grew. Eventually, he was asked to cater the reception for President Woodrow Wilson's wedding to his second wife, Edith in 1916. Boiardi opened his own restaurant in Cleveland, Ohio and noticed that diners often wanted food to just take home with them, so Boiardi started a company, producing sauce and spaghetti in cans. Because his own sales staff had trouble pronouncing his last name, he put the phonetic spelling on the label: Chef Boy-Ar-Dee. The chef helped spaghetti become one of America's favorite foods. During World War II, Chef Boyardee was the largest supplier of rations for the U.S. and Allied Forces.

Amadeo Pietro "Peter" Giannini was born in 1870. The son of an immigrant from Liguria in Northern Italy, his first name was given to him as a reminder of the old country. His second name was given to him as an "American" name. Giannini saw his father killed as a child. His mother remarried, and Giannini worked for his stepfather in his North Beach wholesale produce business. He noticed that regular banks did not want to give loans to Italian immigrant farmers, so he used family capital to start his own bank in San Francisco's North Beach in 1904. Giannini's Banca d'Italia (Bank of Italy) opened in what was once a saloon. Giannini personally greeted each customer and lent money to people based on judgment of their character. In 1919, he innovated the branch banking system. In 1928, Giannini bought a New York bank called Bank of America, and he used that name for his network of banks. Giannini lived to see his network become the largest bank in the United States with its headquarters in the TransAmerica building in San Francisco. Giannini financed the Golden Gate Bridge, the fledgling film industry, including Cecil B. DeMille's *The Ten Commandments*, and Walt Disney's *Snow White*, as well as California's aerospace and agricultural industries.

In 1906, Guiseppe Uddo emigrated from Sicily to New Orleans, Louisiana. With another family, he built a business by selling vegetables they picked by hand, then canning tomatoes and vegetables and selling the canned goods. This became the Progresso Company, which is still in business today, selling canned soups and other products.

Brothers Ernest and Julio Gallo used their life savings of $5,000 at the end of Prohibition and began producing wine from the vineyards their father had owned in California. In their first year of business, they made a profit of $34,000. They also helped to launch California's wine industry. Today, more than 100 wineries in the United States are owned by Italian Americans.

Born in Genoa, Andrea Sbarbaro, went to San Francisco as a young man in 1852. He believed in education and opened a night school for Italian immigrants and even wrote textbooks for them to work from. His first success came as a banker. Then, in 1881, with his wealth, Sbarbaro bought land in Sonoma County, California, and called it Asti after a grape-growing region in northern Italy. When he started his company, Sbarbaro believed in a fair system in which each worker would hold a share of stock in the company; however, he soon discovered workers did not want to deduct the cost of a share from their wages. The first years of cultivating the land were difficult. There were insect attacks and flooding, but in the end Sbarbaro introduced new plants that had never been grown in the region before. Oranges, limes, pomegranates, chestnuts, and olives flourished on the land. Sbarbaro built the Italian Swiss Colony, which today is a wine empire.

Anthony Rossi began Tropicana as a Florida fruit-packaging company in 1947. In 1954, Rossi innovated a pasteurization process for orange juice. Consumers could now have not-from-concentrate orange juice in a ready-to-serve package for the first time. In 1978, Rossi sold his company to Beatrice Foods, and, in 1998, PepsiCo, bought the company. Today, Tropicana produces more fruit juice than any other company in the world. Its juices are sold in 23 countries, and its sales equal $2.5 billion annually.

With a $2,500 loan, Jeno Paulucci started Chun King Chow Mein in 1946. Twenty years later, he sold the company for $63 million in cash. Paulucci has also launched Jeno's Pizza Rolls, Luigino's Inc, a line of frozen pasta entrees, and Pasta Lovers Trattorias.

Two Italian Americans founded the best-known submarine sandwich chains in the United States. Anthony Conza founded the first Blimpie in New Jersey in 1975. Today, there are more than 2,000 Blimpies in the United States and in 13 foreign countries worth a total of $38 million. At age 17,

Notable Italian–American Women

Mother Cabrini (1850–1917) Sister Francesca Cabrini was born in Lombardy, Italy, on July 15, 1850. She founded the Missionary Sisters of the Sacred Heart in 1887. Sister Cabrini arrived in New York in 1889 to help Italian immigrants. She became an American citizen in 1909 and founded 14 American colleges, 98 schools, 28 orphanages, 8 hospitals, and other institutions with more than 4,000 recruited sisters. Sister Cabrini died in 1917 and became the first American to be canonized a saint in 1946.

Geraldine A. Ferraro (1935–) The first woman vice presidential nominee in the United States was born in New York on August 26, 1935, the daughter of an Italian immigrant father and a seamstress. In school, Ferraro skipped three grades and finished high school at 16. While teaching in public schools, she attended law school at night. Ferraro became an assistant district attorney in Queens, New York, in 1974. Four years later, she headed the Special Victims Bureau. There, she prosecuted cases of child abuse, domestic violence, and rape. She was then elected to the U.S. House of Representatives for the State of New York and served as a representative from 1979 to 1985.

Penny Marshall (1942–) Carole Penny Masciarelli went to the University of New Mexico, where she earned degrees in math and psychology. Her brother Gary gave Marshall her first film role in 1968. Marshall's big moment came when Gary cast her as Laverne in a *Happy Days* episode. Laverne and her friend Shirley were a hit, and Gary developed a show around the characters. *Laverne and Shirley* ran from 1978 to 1983. Marshall then directed *The Tracey Ullman Show,* and such films as *Jumpin' Jack Flash*, *Big* (making her the first woman in history to direct a film that earned $100 million), *Awakenings*, and *A League of Their Own.*

Betty DellaCorte (1933–) Betty DellaCorte is responsible for establishing one of the first shelters for battered women and treatment programs in the nation. Her Faith House Agencies, begun in 1974 in Glendale, Arizona, have helped more than 30,000 women and children. DellaCorte has published two books about her experiences.

Madonna (1958–) Born Madonna Louise Veronica Ciccone on August 16, 1958 in Bay City, Michigan. After studying dance at the University of Michigan, she moved to New York City and studied with noted choreographer Alvin Ailey. Her first mainstream pop hit, "Holiday," reached the Top 20 in the United States in 1983. The single "Like A Virgin," released in 1984, provided Madonna with the first of 11 number one hit singles in the United States. Madonna has won five Grammy awards and a Best Actress Golden Globe for the film *Evita.* In 2000, she married British film director Guy Ritchie and has two children, Lourdes Maria Ciccone Leon and Rocco Ritchie.

Fred De Luca borrowed $1,000 to open his first sandwich shop. There are now over 13,000 Subway Sandwich shops in 64 countries. The company is worth $3 billion.

Italian Americans have found success in every way possible. They have been honored as Nobel Prize winners and Oscar winners and serve in all forms of government. By the end of the twentieth century, about 8 percent, or 82 of the mayors of the 1,056 major U.S. cities had Italian last names. Per state, the largest percentages of mayors are in New York (35 percent), Connecticut (31 percent), and New Jersey (23 percent). Six of the Italian-American mayors are women. At the close of the twentieth century, 31 men and women of Italian descent were serving as members of the U.S. Congress.

Over the years, Italian Americans have contributed innovations to the way we live. For example, an Italian immigrant to New Jersey named Italo Marcioni invented the ice cream cone in 1896.

Alessandro Dandini, who came to the United States in 1945, patented more than 22 inventions in his lifetime. His work included the three-way light bulb, the rigid retractable automobile top, and the spherical system, which concentrates and extracts solar energy.

Thanks to Bernard Cousino the world has the eight-track tape player and the automobile tape deck. Cousino held more than 76 patents on audiovisual equipment. In 1994, just days before his death, he filed yet another patent—this time for a continuous loop videocassette that allows VCRs to play tapes repeatedly without rewinding.

The Jacuzzi family is responsible for bringing the world the Jacuzzi hot tub and spa. The family of seven sons and six daughters came to America in 1907. They formed Jacuzzi Brothers Incorporated in 1915 and supplied the American military with propellers. In 1926, they invented the deep well (jet) water pump, which led to the popular whirlpool bath.

In 1967, Jim Delligatti, owner of a McDonald's franchise in

Pittsburgh, Pennsylvania, came up with the Big Mac. The sandwich is now a McDonald's classic. Worldwide more than 14 billion Big Macs have been sold, making it the world's most popular sandwich.

FOOD BUSINESS

Food became a business in which immigrants could have great success. Food was also a way to keep families together. In fact, family dinners are still an important tradition in many Italian-American families. It is because of Italian immigrants that people in the United States today regularly enjoy foods such as spaghetti, lasagna, pizza, ravioli, salami, mozzarella, parmesan, artichokes, zucchini, broccoli, and cauliflower. Food is a big part of festas. These sometimes weeklong festivals are one way in which Italians celebrate and share their pride with people of all races.

Some popular Italian foods can be enjoyed at the Feast of San Gennaro in New York, the oldest and largest festa celebrated in the United States today. It is held for 11 days in September and during that time attracts more than 3 million people. The festival, which began in 1926, is held along Mulberry Street in what remains of Little Italy located in lower Manhattan. The festival's most popular feature is the food. People might be serving sausage stacked with sliced onions and green peppers sizzling on a grill. Other festival fun includes carnival games and entertainment. Festas occur all over the nation. There is Festa Italiana in Milwaukee, the Mount Carmel Feast in Rhode Island, Our Lady of Mt. Carmel Festival in Chicago, St. Anthony's Italian-American Festival in Delaware, Villa Rosa in Maryland, St. Andrew's Feast in Connecticut, and more.

ASSIMILATION

Between 1880 and 1920, almost 4 million Italians immigrated to the United States. They faced hardship, prejudice, and discrimination. They tried to stay true to their Italian traditions,

Italian culture has made rich contributions to the American diet. Foods like pasta, pizza, mozzarella, provolone, broccoli, and zucchini all find their origins in Italian cooking. It was an Italian American, Jim Delligatti, who invented the Big Mac!

but by the end of World War II began hiding their cultural identity. Today, Italian Americans constitute about 6 percent of the U.S. population—an estimated, 15,942,683 Italian Americans—and they are proud of their heritage. The states with the largest populations of Italian-Americans are Rhode Island with 202,735; Connecticut with 653,386; New Jersey with 1,518,331; New York with 2,727,534; Massachusetts

The Feast of San Gennaro in New York City is the oldest and largest feast (or *festa*) of its kind in America. Begun in 1926, the tradition continues to be celebrated on New York's Mulberry Street and features delicious food, carnival games, and other entertainment.

with 890,451; Pennsylvania with 1,497,162; and California with 1,411,054.

Because of assimilation, many of the Italian immigrant neighborhoods with their shops and cultural flavor have disappeared. But many Italian Americans are now rediscovering their roots and many have kept Italian traditions alive through-out the generations that their families have been in America.

Italians came to escape the threat of poverty. When they arrived, they were handed picks, axes, and shovels and told to build America. Through hard work and perseverance, Italian Americans did exactly that. They helped the United States grow as a nation and added to its cultural diversity.

1492   Columbus discovers America.

1497   Giovanni Caboto (John Cabot) reaches what is now the United States.

1499   Amerigo Vespucci sails to the New World in 1499, landing in what is now Brazil.

1504   The southern portion of the Italian peninsula and the island of Sicily are a fiefdom belonging to Spanish princes; Spanish rule remains dominant in the South for 200 years.

1657   Seeking escape from religious persecution, the first group of Italian immigrants comes to New York, settling in the Dutch colony of New Amsterdam.

1804   Emperor of France, Napoleon Bonaparte, puts his brother on the throne of a Kingdom of Italy; however, this kingdom is short-lived.

1805   Giuseppe Mazzini is born in Genoa.

1807   Giuseppe Garibaldi is born on July 4 in Nice.

1831   Mazzini creates patriotic movement known as Young Italy.

1848   Mazzini returns to Milan, Italy, after exile, hoping that an Italian nation is about to be born.

1848   California Gold Rush begins; Italian immigrants come to California and settle in San Francisco.

1849   *L'Eco d'Italia,* the first Italian language newspaper in the United States, begins publication.

1855   Castle Garden landing station is opened for immigrants entering the United States.

1859   Austria declares war on Piedmont-Sardinia.

1861   Victor Emmanuel becomes ruler of the Kingdom of Italy, formalizing unification.

1871   The pope gives up Rome, except for Vatican City, and Rome becomes Italy's capital.

1880   Italians begin four decades of migration to the United States; they are stopped only by changes in U.S. immigration laws in 1924 and by the new Italian Fascist government, which allows few people to leave the country.

1885   U.S. Congress enacts contract labor laws, making it illegal to recruit foreign workers before they reach the United States.

1885–1887	U.S. Government passes laws banning people from entering the country who might become "public charges."
1890	The United States federal government takes over the immigration process; October, 11, Italian Americans killed in New Orleans lynching.
1892	Ellis Island opens its doors.
1902	The Passenger Act is passed as attempt to make conditions for immigrants traveling on oceanliners to the United States more bearable.
1912	Arturo Giovannitti and Guiseppe Ettor lead strike in Lawrence, Massachusetts; the strike is a turning point for labor unions across the nation.
1914	World War I begins; strike by the United Mine Workers against John D. Rockefeller, Jr's., Colorado Fuel and Iron Company Works; 45 people die in blaze.
1916	Fiorello La Guardia wins congressional seat.
1920	Sacco and Vanzetti trial.
1924	U.S. immigration laws are completely revised, limiting numbers of Italian Americans allowed into the country.
1927	Sacco and Vanzetti die by electrocution.
1934	La Guardia begins first of three consecutive terms as mayor of New York City.
1936	Mussolini allies himself with Nazi Germany.
1941	Japan attacks Pearl Harbor, bringing the United States into World War II.
1942	In January, all enemy aliens are required to register at their local post office. In October, Italian immigrants are released from the relocation program.
1950s	Italian-American singers top the American charts.

BIBLIOGRAPHY

BOOKS

Coan, Peter. *Ellis Island Interviews: In Their Own Words.* New York: Facts on File, 1997.

Di Franco, J. Philip. *The Italian Americans.* Philadelphia: Chelsea House, 1988.

DiStasi, Lawrence. *Dream Streets: The Big Book of Italian American Culture.* New York: Harper & Row, 1989.

Hoobler, Dorothy, and Thomas Hoobler. *The Italian American Family Album.* New York: Oxford University Press, 1994.

Laurino, Maria. *Were You Always an Italian?: Ancestors and Other Icons of Italian America.* New York: W.W. Norton, 2001.

Lee, Kathleen. *Tracing Our Italian Roots.* Santa Fe, NM: John Muir Publications, 1993.

Mangione, Jerre, and Ben Morreale. *La Storia: Five Centuries of the Italian American Experience.* New York: HarperCollins, 1992.

Parrino, Maria, ed. *Italian American Autobiographies.* Providence, RI: Italian Americana Publications, 1993.

Stave, Bruce M., and John Sutherland. *From the Old Country: An Oral History of European Migration to America.* New York: Maxwell Macmillan, 1994.

Todd, Anne M. *Italian Immigrants: 1880–1920* (Coming to America). Mankato, MN.: Blue Earth Books, 2002.

VIDEO

Italians in America: The Journey. Produced by Greystone Communications, Inc., for A & E Network. Producers Craig Haffner and Donna E. Lusitana. Writer/Director Laura Verklan, 1998.

Italians in America: Home. Produced by Greystone Communications, Inc., for A & E Network. Producers Craig Haffner and Donna E. Lusitana. Writer/Director Laura Verklan, 1998.

NONFICTION

Cappello, Mary. *Night Bloom: A Memoir.* Beacon Press, 1998.

Cateura, Linda Brandi. *Growing Up Italian: Memoirs of 24 Celebrated Italian-Americans.* iUniverse.com, January 2001.

Esposito, Russell R. *The Golden Milestone: Over 2500 Years of Italian Contributions to Civilization,* 2nd ed. New York Learning Library, 2002.

Ets, Marie Hall. *Rosa: The Life of an Italian Immigrant.* (Wisconsin Studies in Autobiography). Madison: University of Wisconsin Press, 1999.

Lagumina, Salvatore J. *WOP!* (Essay Series 32) Guernica Editions, May 1999.

Laurino, Maria. *Were You Always an Italian?: Ancestors and Other Icons of Italian America.* New York: W.W. Norton, June 2001.

Luconi, Stefano. *From Paesani to White Ethnics: The Italian Experience in Philadelphia* (SUNY Series in Italian American Culture). Albany: State University of New York Press, 2001.

Mangione, Jerre, and Ben Morreale. *La Storia: Five Centuries of the Italian American Experience.* New York: HarperCollins, 1992.

Mangione, Jerre Gerlando, and Eugene Paul Nassar. *Mount Allegro: A Memoir of Italian American Life.* Syracuse: Syacuse University Press, 1998.

Morreale, Ben and Robert Carola. *Italian Americans: The Immigrant Experience* (Immigrant Experience Series). Westport, CT: Hugh Lauter Levin Associates, 2000.

Radomile, Leon J. *Heritage Italian-American Style.* Novato, CA: Vincero Enterprises, November 1999.

Schiavelli, Vincent. *Bruculinu, America: Remembrances of Sicilian-American Brooklyn, Told in Stories and Recipes.* New York: Houghton Mifflin, 1998.

FICTION

Ardizzone, Tony. *In the Garden of Papa Santuzzu.* New York: Picador USA, 1999.

Cusumano, Camille. *The Last Cannoli.* Brooklyn, NY: Legas, 1999.

Ermelino, Louisa. *The Sisters Mallone: Una Storia Di Famiglia.* New York: Simon & Schuster, 2002.

Puzo, Mario. *The Fortunate Pilgrim.* New York: Random House, 1997.

Il Circolo Calabrese
www.circolocalabrese.org

Italian American Heritage Foundation
http://www.iahfsj.org

The Italian–American Web Site of New York
www.italian-american.com/main.htm

The Italians of New York: Five Centuries of Struggle and Achievement
http://www.nyhistory.org/italians

The National Italian American Foundation
http://www.niaf.org

Una Storia Segreta: When Italian Americans Were "Enemy Aliens"
http://www.io.com/~segreta/index.html

VirtualItalia.com
http://www.virtualitalia.com

American Italian Historical Association
209 Flagg Place
Staten Island, NY 10304

Center for Immigration Studies
1522 K Street NW, Suite 820
Washington, D.C. 20005-1202

Ellis Island Library
Statue of Liberty National Monument
One Liberty Island
New York, NY 10004

The Italian Historical Society of America
111 Columbia Heights
Brooklyn, NY 11201

National Italian American Foundation
1860 19th Street NW
Washington, D.C. 20009

"My America" text on page 37 from **Ellis Island Interviews** by Peter Morton Coan. Copyright © 1997 by Peter Morton Coan. Reprinted by permission of Facts on File, Inc.

REBECCA ALDRIDGE has been an editor and writer for more than seven years. In addition to this title, she has written books on Thomas Jefferson and the presidency as well as a six-book series on simple machines. Her editorial work includes input on more than fifty children's nonfiction books on a wide variety of topics. She lives in Minneapolis, Minnesota.

DANIEL PATRICK MOYNIHAN is a former United States senator from New York. He is also the only person in American history to have served in the cabinets or subcabinets of four successive presidents—Kennedy, Johnson, Nixon, and Ford. Formerly a professor of government at Harvard University, he has written and edited many books.